Heritage Language Development

Also by Language Education Associates:

Foreign Language Education the Easy Way
Stephen D. Krashen

The Case for Late Intervention: Once a Good Reader, Always a Good Reader
Stephen D. Krashen and Jeff McQuillan

Under Attack: The Case Against Bilingual Education
Stephen D. Krashen

Every Person a Reader:
An Alternative to the California Task Force Report on Reading
Stephen D. Krashen

For more information contact:
Language Education Associates
Post Office Box 3141
Culver City, California 90231-3141
USA

Toll Free (US & Canada): (800) 200-8008
Fax: +1 (310) 568-9040

e-mail: input@LanguageBooks.com
http://www.LanguageBooks.com

Heritage Language Development

Edited by:

Stephen D. Krashen
Lucy Tse
Jeff McQuillan

1998
Language Education Associates
Culver City, California

Heritage Language Development

Language Education Associates
Post Office Box 3141
Culver City, California 90231 USA
www.LanguageBooks.com

Publisher's Cataloging-in-Publication
(Provided by Quality Books, Inc.)

Heritage language development/ edited by Stephen Krashen, Lucy
        Tse, Jeff McQuillan. -- 1st ed.
        p. cm.
        Includes bibliographical references.
        Preassigned LCCN: 98-65397
        ISBN: 0-9652808-4-5

        1. Education, Bilingual. 2. Multicultural education. 3.
        Sociolinguistics. 4. Second language acquisition. I.
        Krashen, Stephen D. II. Tse, Lucy. III. McQuillan, Jeff.

        LC3715.H47 1998   370.117'5
                                                 QBI98-454

Additional copies of this publication are available for $16.00 (US) plus $3.00 for shipping within North America. CA residents please add 8.25% sales tax.
Orders may be sent to: Language Education Associates, PO Box 3141, Culver City, CA 90231-3141 USA.   Fax: +1 (310) 568-9040.

Credit cards and purchase orders are welcome
Prices are subject to change without notice.

PRINTED IN THE UNITED STATES OF AMERICA

Contents

Introduction

Introduction

Heritage language (HL) development appears to be an excellent investment. For a small effort, for example optional classes in popular literature and social studies in the primary language, the payoffs are enormous.

In Chapter 1, Krashen argues that developing the first language, assuming that English is also fully developed, is, at worst, harmless. Fishman's work has shown us that multilingualism is not related to political unrest or to economic problems. There are also benefits: those who develop their first language in addition to English do slightly better economically as well as academically. In addition, there is some evidence that multilingualism may be good for our trade deficit—knowing the language of your customer is good for business.

In chapter 2, Tse points out that some members of minority cultures pass through several stages:

(1) Unawareness of ethnic differences.

(2) Ethnic Ambivalence/Evasion. In this stage, ethnic minorities prefer assimilation into the mainstream group, and prefer the use of English.

(3) Ethnic Emergence, a period of identity exploration, resulting for some in a preference for the ethnic group over the mainstream, which could be caused by the experience of prejudice and/or exposure to issues of ethnicity.

(4) Ethnic Identity Incorporation, in which ethnic minorities resolve many of their conflicts about ethnicity and find membership in the minority American group.

Proficiency in the heritage language can facilitate movement through stage (3) and into the desirable stage (4).

Wong Fillmore's work has sensitized us to problems heritage language speakers can have when their competence is low and communication difficulties develop with members of the family. In chapter 3, Cho and Krashen present research that confirms this, showing that the problem extends to members of the extended family and community. In chapter

4, Krashen discusses a related problem, a special case of language shyness that HL speakers sometimes experience because of expectations others have of their HL competence. This shyness results in less input and even less competence.

Heritage languages are very hard to maintain: Language shift is powerful. In chapter 5, Tse shows that some heritage language programs have been successful, particularly those that are integrated into the school day.

In chapter 6, McQuillan describes heritage language classes based on extensive reading that not only succeeded, but provided a foundation for future progress. Students made progress and developed an interest in reading in their HL.

In chapter 7, Shin and Krashen present data suggesting that good HL programs are supported. Parents, teachers and administrators agree that bilingualism has real advantages, it is a good idea to maintain the first culture, and that developing the first language will help in maintaining the first culture.

Thus, HL development has practical advantages, prevents some serious communication problems, may ease movement into a very positive stage of identity development, and can be done comfortably. In addition, its advantages seem to be understood by parents, teachers, and administrators.

Finally, we need to mention another advantage of heritage language development, one not covered in any of the papers in this volume: It can help relieve the shortage of bilingual teachers. We can grow our own.

Our studies, however, leave gaps. Tse and McQuillan's research has provided us with a beginning in methodology, but we need to know if developing the HL will actually have the effects we predict it will: Can HL programs result in practical benefits, less language shyness, better communication with other HL speakers and movement through Tse's stages? We have, in other words, made the case that HL development results in these advantages, but we now need to show that successful HL programs can "deliver the goods".

1. Heritage Language Development: Some Practical Arguments

Stephen Krashen

Heritage Languages are Hard to Maintain

A heritage language is one not spoken by the dominant culture, but is spoken in the family or associated with the heritage culture. According to common knowledge, immigrants are reluctant to give up their heritage languages, and prefer to keep them rather than acquire English.

In Krashen (1996) I reviewed a number of studies that showed that just the opposite is true: heritage languages are typically not maintained and are rarely developed. They are, in fact, victims of language shift, a powerful process that favors the language of the country over the language of the family.

Table 1 presents one of the studies from this review. Hudson-Edwards and Bills (1980) reported more competence in English than Spanish among younger Mexican-Americans living in a Spanish-speaking community in Albuquerque, while older Mexican Americans reported bet-

Table 1

Self-report of Ability in Spanish and English

(Percentage Claiming "Good" or "Very Good" Ability)

Generation	Spanish Ability	English Ability
Junior [a]	33% (26/80)	81% (69/81)
Senior [b]	85% (74/87)	47% (41/88)

[a]Junior: children of heads of households

[b]Senior: heads of households, spouses, siblings

ter Spanish. Even among the older subjects, however, nearly half described their English competence as "good" or "very good."

Baratz-Snowden, Rock, Pollack and Wilder (1988) provide confirming data. Parents of language minority students rated themselves as more competent in their primary language, but rated their children as more competent in English. Table 2 presents data on three of the five groups they studied (for Asian, n = 866; for Mexican American, n = 891; for Cuban, n = 502).

Table 2
Parents' Ratings of English and Heritage Language Ability

A. PERCENT RATING THEMSELVES AND THEIR CHILDREN AS SPEAKING, UNDERSTANDING, READING AND WRITING ENGLISH AS "VERY WELL" OR "WELL"

Group	Parents	Children
Asian	74.0%	88.5%
Mexican-American	54.0%	86.5%
Cuban	51.0%	97%

B. RATINGS OF HERITAGE LANGUAGE COMPETENCE: PERCENT RATING THEIR LITERACY AND THEIR CHILDREN'S COMPETENCE AS "VERY GOOD" OR "GOOD"

Group	Parents	Children
Asian	84.0%	32.0%
Mexican-American	59.0%	34.0%
Cuban	97.0%	79.0%

Confirming the universality of language shift, Langan (1993) studied the language ability of 399 speakers of K'iche' in a community in Guatemala that was considered to be linguistically conservative; they were known to be resisting the shift from K'iche', their heritage language, to Spanish. Nearly 90% of the sample agreed or strongly agreed with the statement "it is important to the K'ichi' people to keep their own language and culture."

Table 3 presents self-ratings for Spanish and K'iche'. While those with less education regard themselves as better in their heritage language, those with seven years or more of schooling rate themselves slightly higher in Spanish.

Table 3
Mean Ratings of K'iche' Speakers in K'iche' and Spanish

Educational Level	K'iche'	Spanish
Low (0-6 years)	3.55	2.12
High (7 yrs or more)	3.06	3.30

Ratings: 1 = not at all; 4 = very well

Investigation of language use patterns gave similar results. Those with more education actually reported more Spanish use with peers and a considerable amount of Spanish use with family members (table 4).

Table 4
Language Use Among K'iche' Speakers

Educational level	Mother	Grandmother	Peer
Low	1.02	1.06	1.50
High	2.11	2.02	2.95

1 = always K'iche'; 4 = always Spanish

Subjects were clearly aware that language shift was taking place. About 25% agreed or strongly agreed that "many K'ichi' children have difficulty understanding when their parents speak to them in K'ichi'" and about half agreed or strongly agreed that "Spanish is more important than K'iche' for children living in my house to know."

Thus, despite strong feelings that K'ichi' was important to them, a significant part of the group felt more competent in Spanish (about 1/3 were in the high education group), used it more among peers, and there was clear recognition that shift was occurring.

The Value of Heritage Languages

Should we care about the loss of heritage languages? Some, in fact, feel that heritage language loss is a good thing, that bilingualism can lead to divisiveness and political unrest. We need, it is asserted, "the glue of language to help hold us together" (Robert Dole, quoted in the Los Angeles Times, October 31, 1995). Additionally, it is claimed that bilingualism decreases the individual's chances of success. Gingrich (1995) asserts that "Immigrants need to make a sharp break with the past ..." (p. A9).

MULTILINGUALISM AND THE NATIONAL WELL-BEING

Maintenance of the heritage language does not appear to play a role in the health of nations. Fishman (1990) analyzed the impact of 230 possible predictors of civil strife and economic well-being in 170 countries. His results suggest that multilingualism is not to blame for political or economic problems.

In Fishman's study, civil strife was defined as a combination of factors, such as "magnitude and frequency of conspiracy against the established government ... internal warfare ... (and) internal turmoil (riots, strikes and protests)." Fishman found thirteen significant predictors of civil strife, but linguistic heterogeneity was not one of them. The simple correlation of linguistic heterogeneity and civil strife was a low .21, which meant that it accounted for only 4% of the variation in civil strife. When other factors were considered, it had no predictive value at all.

Similarly, Fishman found ten significant predictors of per capita gross national product. Once again, linguistic heterogeneity was not among these predictors. The simple correlation of linguistic heterogeneity and gross national product was .32, which means that it accounted for about 10% of the variation in gross national product, but when other factors were considered, it again had no predictive value.

There are, to be sure, multilingual countries with problems; there are also monolingual countries with problems. Fishman's study strongly suggests that multilingualism cannot be blamed for civil strife or lack of economic development.

HERITAGE LANGUAGE DEVELOPMENT AND THE BALANCE OF TRADE

"Sir, the most useful international language in the world is not necessarily English, but rather it is the language of your client." (J. Kolbert, cited in Simon, 1988 p. 27).

Those experienced in international trade tell us that if you want to buy, you can do it in your own language, but if you want to sell, it is a good idea to know your customer's language. The results of a study by Fishman, Cooper and Rosenbaum are consistent with this wisdom: Exporting (selling) is related to language use, but importing (buying) is not.

Fishman et al. (1977) studied factors related to the spread of English in 102 countries, and reported that the more a country supplies English-speaking countries with goods, the more use of English there is in that country. More importing from English-speaking countries did not mean more English use. This suggests that more knowledge of English results in more exporting to English-speaking countries.[1]

If language competence does influence trade, this is a strong argument for the development of foreign languages and heritage languages in particular: The better we know other languages, the better chance there is to sell to countries that use those languages. Heritage language speakers could thus be an important natural resource: Nurturing and developing heritage languages may be a good thing for the economy and the balance of trade.

Bilingualism and Individual Well-Being

Bilingualism seems to have no negative effects on the individual's ability to function in society. In studies done in the United States, it has been concluded that as long as English language development occurs, continued heritage language development is related to superior scholastic achievement with no socioeconomic disadvantages.

SCHOOL SUCCESS

Fernandez and Nielsen (1986) concluded that "proficiency in Spanish ... has a positive effect on achievement" (p. 60). In their study of Hispanic high school seniors, they reported that those with exposure to Spanish (classified as "bilingual" regardless of how much exposure they had

Table 5
Heritage Language Proficiency and School Success

		Bilingual	Monolingual
	n	1876	474
Expectations*		15	14
English Reading Test Scores		48	45
English Vocab Test Scores		48	46

*Expectations = Years of Schooling Expected to Complete
from: Fernandez and Nielsen, 1986

had) did better than monolingual Hispanics in English reading and had higher educational expectations (expected to complete more years of school), as shown in table 5.

In a regression analysis using only the bilingual sample, Fernandez and Nielsen reported that degree of Spanish proficiency was a significant predictor of educational expectations and English vocabulary. In addition, there was no relationship between Spanish proficiency and English reading, confirming that greater Spanish proficiency was not related to lower English reading performance. Spanish proficiency was, in fact, a slightly stronger predictor of educational expectations than English proficiency was.

Nielsen and Lerner (1986) arrived at a similar conclusion from a slightly different analysis of the same data set, obtaining a significantly positive relationship between "Hispanicity" (a combination of measures of Spanish use with parents and Spanish ability) and educational attainment and expectations, controlling for SES, scores on tests of reading, vocabulary, and mathematics, and years of residence in the United States.

Garcia (1985) used a different sample, 1500 Chicano college students, and his conclusions confirm that heritage language maintenance is not a problem but is, rather, an advantage: Fluency in the heritage language was positively related to self-esteem, more ambitious plans for the future, confidence in achieving goals, and the amount of control subjects felt they had over their lives. All these variables, as well as fluency, were, in addition, positively related to grade point average. All subjects in this study reported very high competence in English. Huang (1995) reported similar results: Mexican American eighth graders who described themselves as biliterate had higher self-confidence than monoliterates (Spanish or English), controlling for sociodemographic background and school experience.

It needs to be emphasized that these studies do not show that students who develop their first language and who do not develop English do well in school. They show, rather, that development of the heritage language makes a contribution to school success, once English is acquired.

OCCUPATIONAL STATUS

Tienda and Neidert (1984) analyzed predictors of occupational status among Hispanic men in the labor force in 1975, ages 18–64. Education was a clear predictor of occupational status, as was English language ability. Not surprisingly, those who spoke only Spanish or who spoke Spanish as their dominant language did not have as high occupational status as English-dominant bilinguals. Of interest to us, however, is the finding that English-dominant bilinguals were slightly better off than those who spoke only English. This language variable was not anywhere near as strong as the education variable, but the analysis confirmed that bilingualism is not harmful and can be beneficial, as long as English has been acquired.

Bilingualism is thus of no harm to the individual. Retention of the heritage language, in fact, appears to be related to better school success and slightly higher occupational status. There are, to be sure, bilinguals who do poorly in school and in their occupations, but there appear to be more who do well.

OTHER ADVANTAGES

The arguments presented here have been practical: Development of the heritage language, it has been argued, is not harmful for nations, and may have important trade advantages. As long as the dominant language is acquired, it is harmless to the individual and may even be beneficial. There are other advantages of heritage language development that do not obviously translate into dollars and cents but appear, nevertheless, to be very important: Heritage language development can facilitate communication with elders and the heritage language community, allowing the heritage language speaker to profit from their wisdom and knowledge (Wong Fillmore, 1991; Cho, Cho and Tse, 1997; Cho and Krashen, this volume). It may also help promote a healthy sense of multiculturalism, an acceptance not only of both the majority and heritage culture, but a deeper understanding of the human condition.

Developing Heritage Languages

If we want to maintain and develop heritage languages, we should try to understand why they are lost, even when communities want to hold on the them. There are significant barriers to heritage language development:

(1) Lack of input, in the form of interaction, books, and other forms of media.

(2) The desire to fully integrate into the target culture, with rejection of the heritage culture, a stage many minority group members go through (Tse, this volume).

(3) Ridicule and correction when the heritage language is used by more competent heritage language speakers, resulting in a reluctance to use the language and less input (Krashen, this volume).

(4) Poor heritage language teaching programs.

Barriers (1), (3) and (4) can be dealt with when we set up heritage classes that provide the input students need in a non-threatening environment. McQuillan (1996, this volume) has shown how this can be done, as heritage language classes that focus on popular literature and encourage free voluntary reading, a modest investment that can have a tremendous payoff for the individual and society.

Note

1. Their composite measure of the spread of English in a country included the use of English as an official language, as a language of government administration, as a technical language, the degree to which English was taught and used in the schools and universities, newspapers, TV and radio in English, and the use of English as a lingua franca (language of communication).

I list below only a few of the predictor variables investigated:

—Communicability, rated on a four point scale. The lowest rating was given to countries in which the most widely spoken language was used in parts of the country only. The highest rating was given to countries using a language spoken in more than three other countries.

—Economic development, including per capita GNP, life expectancy, and infant mortality.

—Urbanization, the percentage of the population living in urban areas.

—Literacy and educational attainment.

—Imports and exports, including total imports and exports and imports from and exports to English-speaking countries (relative importance of English-speaking countries as suppliers and customers, rated on a nine-point scale).

—Political and religious affiliation.

The results are presented below:

<u>Multiple Regression Analysis: Predictors of English Use</u>

step	variable	r	r2
1	Former Anglophone Colony	.77	.57
2	Exports to English-speaking Countries	.38	.67
3	Communicability of Language of Largest Mother-tongue Group	.42	.71

from: Fishman et. al., table 16.

Here is an explanation of this table. First, all three of the variables listed made independent contributions to predicting the spread of English. Specifically, countries that were former colonies of English speaking countries were likely to use English a great deal, as were countries that exported a larger percentage of their goods to English speaking countries, as were countries in which one local language did not predominate. None of the other of the 50 variables Fishman et. al. included made a significant contribution. Second, knowledge of these three predictors provides us with about 71% of the information needed to predict the use of English in a country (r_2 = 71%).

These results could, of course, also mean that more exporting to English-speaking countries stimulates more English-language use, but this is unlikely. It is more likely that those countries that use English more (because of their status as former colonies and need for English because of linguistic diversity) have more competence in English, and thus are able to negotiate with English-speaking countries better. It is hard to imagine how exporting could lead to greater internal use of English in a non-English speaking country, other than as a language to be taught.

References

Baratz-Snowden, J., Rock, D., Pollack, J. and Wilder, G. (1988) *Parent Preference Study*. Princeton, NJ: Educational Testing Service.

Cho, G., Cho, K-S., and Tse, L. 1997. "Why ethnic minorities want to develop their heritage language: The case of Korean Americans." *Language, Culture and Curriculum*. 10(2): 106-112.

Fernandez, R. and Nielsen, F. (1986) "Bilingualism and Hispanic scholastic achievement: Some baseline results." *Social Science Research* **15**: 43–70.

Fishman, J. (1990) "Empirical explorations of two popular assumptions: Inter-polity perspective on the relationships between linguistic hetero-geneity, civil strife, and per capita gross national product." In G. Imhoff (Ed.), *Learning in Two Languages*. New Brunswick, NJ: Transaction Publishers. pp. 209–225.

Fishman, J., Cooper, R. and Rosenbaum, Y. (1977) "English the world over: A factor in the creation of bilingualism today." In P. Hornby (Ed.), *Bilingualism: Psychological, Social and Educational Implications*. New York: Academic Press. pp. 103–109.

Garcia, H. (1985) "Family and offspring language maintenance and their effects of Chicano college students' confidence and grades." In E. Garcia and R. Padilla (Eds.), *Advances in Bilingual Education Research*. Tucson: University of Arizona Press. pp. 226–243.

Gingrich, N. (1995) "English literacy is the coin of the realm." *Los Angeles Times*, August 4, 1995, p. B9.

Huang, G.G. (1995) "Self-reported biliteracy and self-esteem: A study of Mexican-American 8th graders." *Applied Psycholinguistics* **16**: 271–291.

Hudson-Edwards, A. and Bills, G. (1980) "Intergenerational language shift in an Albuquerque barrio." In E. Blansitt and R. Teschner (Eds.), *A Festschrift for Jacob Ornstein*. New York: Newbury House. pp. 139–158.

Krashen, S. (1996) *Under Attack: The Case Against Bilingual Education*. Culver City: Language Education Associates.

Langan, K. (1993) "Ambivalent attitudes in a conservative K'iche' com-munity." *AILA Review* **10**: 7–22.

McQuillan, J. (1996) "How should heritage languages be taught? The effects of a free voluntary reading program." *Foreign Language Annals* **29**: 56–72.

Nielsen, F. and Lerner, S. (1986) "Language skills and school achieve-ment of bilingual Hispanics." *Social Science Research* **15**: 209–240.

Simon, P. (1988) *The Tongue-Tied American*. New York: Continuum.

Tienda, M. and Niedert, L. (1984) "Language, education, and the socioeconomic achievement of Hispanic origin men." *Social Science Quarterly* **65**: 519–536.

Wong Fillmore, L. (1991) "When learning a second language means losing the first." *Early Childhood Research Quarterly* **6**: 323–346.

2. Ethnic Identity Formation and Its Implications for Heritage Language Development

Lucy Tse

A number of researchers have proposed a developmental view of ethnic identity development, suggesting that ethnic minorities (EMs) move through a predictable path when coming to terms with their EM status. One specific group of EMs,"visible" or racial minorities, have distinct physical characteristics signalling them as members of a minority group, making it more difficult for them to blend into mainstream society.

Drawing on previous work (Phinney, 1989; Kim, 1981), I proposed a four-stage model of ethnic identity development based on the experiences of racial minorities that focuses on attitudes toward the heritage and majority languages (Tse, in press-a).[1] This chapter reviews some of the evidence for this developmental model and discusses the likelihood of heritage language development in each stage of identity formation.

The Model

The model of ethnic identity development I have proposed was based on an exploratory study (Tse, in press-a) intended to describe the identity-related experiences of the EMs in that study as well as those in previous investigations. The model integrates components of several other existing models (e.g. Phinney, 1989; Kim, 1981) and consists of four major stages.

Stage 1, Unawareness, is a relatively brief period when EMs are not conscious of their minority status and/or of the subordinate status often associated with it. This stage typically occurs before substantive contact with other ethnic or racial groups, for example, before attending school or leaving an ethnic enclave. Stage 2, Ethnic Ambivalence/Evasion, is characterized by ambivalent or negative feelings toward the ethnic culture and the EM's own association with it, while preferring identification with the dominant societal group. This stage may span a relatively long period, for example, childhood through adolescence, and even through adulthood. Stage 3, Ethnic Emergence, is a time when EMs explore their ethnic heritage after confronting the fact that they are members of an ethnic minority group. In contrast to the previous stage where EMs prefer association with the majority group, the exploration during stage 3 leads some EMs to embrace their ethnic heritage sometimes in favor of the mainstream group. Finally, in stage 4, Ethnic Identity Incorporation, EMs discover and join the ethnic minority American group (e.g. Mexican Americans, Iranian Americans) and resolve many of the ethnic identity conflicts that became salient in the previous stage. Because much of the confusion and uncertainty experienced during stages 2 and 3 are resolved in stage 4, this last stage is characterized by acceptance of oneself as an ethnic minority and by improved self-image.

Limitations of the Model

There are several important qualifications to this proposed model. First, not all racial minorities go through this development process. Some EMs, including many adult immigrants, may never aspire to become a member of the dominant group, and therefore, never go through these four stages. As Giles and Byrne (1982) point out, individuals are more likely to disassociate from a social group in favor of another if they believe that the boundaries between the old group and the new group are easily crossed. If EMs have strong ties to the ethnic culture and/or possess cultural markers that are not easily shed (e.g. an accent in English), joining the dominant group may never be seen as plausible or desirable.

There is at least one additional group of EMs that may not go through this four-stage developmental process. Those EMs raised in settings in which a strong ethnic minority American presence exists—such as that found in some ethnic enclaves—may find identification and membership in the ethnic minority American group early in life. If such membership is positive and satisfactory, then the EM may never feel the need to join a more positively valued group such as the majority group. After all, the desire to assimilate into mainstream society is driven by the desire to be associated with a non-stigmatized group and ultimately to achieve better self-concept. In essence, these EMs move directly from stage 1 to stage 4, although few such cases have been documented in the literature.

Second, not all EMs who go into the developmental process pass through all four stages of the model. That is, it is possible for EMs to remain in stage 2 (or another stage) throughout their lifetime, depending on a number of factors, including the social and cultural environment in which they live.

Finally, although the process appears to have four stages, it is quite possible that the ethnic identity development process does not end with stage 4 and that one's ethnic identity continues to evolve throughout one's lifetime, even after progressing through these stages. Based on the available data in the literature, however, we can only hypothesize a developmental path up to this point.

Components for Heritage Language Acquisition

Considering previous research on ethnic identity formation and second language acquisition, we may posit that there are two components to maintaining and developing the HL: comprehensible input (CI) and "club" or group membership (CM). Comprehensible input refers to linguistic input in the target language that is understandable. If an acquirer receives CI that contains elements that have not yet been acquired, language acquisition will take place, given the proper affective conditions (Krashen, 1985). A substantial number of studies have shown that acquirers who receive more comprehensible aural and/or written input achieve higher proficiency in the target language than their counterparts receiving less input (Krashen, 1985). Research on reading for pleasure ("free voluntary reading"), for example, reveals that written input improves an acquirer's vocabulary knowledge, grammatical accuracy, reading comprehension, writing ability, spelling, and even aural comprehension and oral proficiency (reviewed in Krashen, 1993).

Club or group membership refers to feeling like a member of the target language group. Being a member of a group carries affective benefits and liabilities such as high or low status, prestige, and self-esteem. For this reason, the groups that individuals join are ones that will not only accept their membership, but are also ones which the individual sees as desirable. Since language is one of the most salient markers of group membership, an acquirer is more likely to develop the language if he or she wants to be identified with that group. This chapter will review some of the evidence for the developmental model and discuss the likelihood of HL acquisition in each stage.

Evidence and Implications

A number of studies examining ethnic identity development in EMs provide evidence supportive of the model described above. For the most part, these studies have used qualitative techniques to probe the experiences of adolescent and adult subjects. Below is a review of some of the available studies, both published and unpublished, that analyze the experiences of ethnic minority American informants. Selected results will be discussed under each of the four stages.

STAGE 1: UNAWARENESS

Nature of the Stage

The first stage, Unawareness, is typically brief and, for many EMs, takes place in childhood. Due to its brevity and occurrence at a relatively early age, it is not surprising that the retrospective reporting used in the available studies tell us little about the nature of this period. By virtue of the fact that it is a time when ethnic minorities are unaware that they belong to a minority group and/or that that membership carries with it subordinate and even stigmatized status, little about this period has been recounted by adults. However, there were some signs of this stage in two interview studies with ethnic minority American adults (Tse, in press-a; 1996). The findings suggest that EMs in this stage have little or no awareness of their subordinate ethnic or language minority status.

Maria, an informant who was born and raised in a Southwestern city (Tse, 1996), pointed out that she was immersed in Mexican culture and the Spanish language, and as a child, was not conscious of different majority and minority groups: "Being raised in a household where you speak Spanish and you have Mexican cultural values everyday, I never thought about it, I never had to think about my culture because I was surrounded by my culture. I was surrounded by Spanish things that were influenced by the Spaniards or Mexicans, so I just took things for granted"(p. 10).

Just as Maria never thought about being of Mexican descent during early childhood, Keith, a 25-year-old Chinese American raised in a predominantly White community, recalled that he felt unquestioningly American and had little awareness of being Chinese. He noted that "it wasn't something I thought about really. It never seemed like an issue...we just did American things" (p. 10). Similarly, Chris, a fourth-generation Japanese American stated that "[I was] never brought up to think that I was Japanese. My parents, I think they just wanted me to know where we came from. Basically we were brought up American" (p. 10).

Possibility of Heritage Language Acquisition

Considering that Unawareness is a time when EMs have not yet begun to see themselves as part of a ethnic or language minority group, club membership is not an issue during this period. For this reason, access to comprehensible input may be sufficient for HL acquisition, while not being exposed to CI results in no HL acquisition.

	CI	CM		HL Acquisition
Case 1	Yes	N/A	$\longrightarrow$	Likely
Case 2	No	N/A	$\longrightarrow$	Unlikely

The cases of Lara and Keith, both U.S.-born, exemplify each of these two cases (Tse, in press-a). Lara was raised in a Filipino enclave in central California where the HL was used as a language of daily communication. As a result, Lara received enough CI in her childhood to develop a conversational level of Tagalog. On the other hand, Keith grew up in a predominantly White neighborhood in a Southwestern city with few Chinese speakers. Raised in a non-Chinese speaking home and without Chinese speaking peers, Keith did not receive CI in or out of the home, and for that reason, did not develop any proficiency in the language.

STAGE 2: ETHNIC AMBIVALENCE/EVASION

Nature of the Stage

The unawareness in stage 1 gives way to a period of Ethnic Ambivalence or Evasion, where EMs develop feelings ranging from ambivalence to rejection of the ethnic culture and heritage language, while preferring assimilation into the mainstream American group and the use of the majority language, English. Phinney (1989) found in an interview study of 91 African American, Asian American, and Latino high school students that over half of the EMs were in stage 2 (Phinney uses the terms "diffusion" and "foreclosure"). Those who felt little interest toward the ethnic culture made comments like this one by a Mexican American teenager: "I don't go looking for my culture. I just go by what my parents say to do, and what they tell me to do..." (p. 44). Indicative of more negative feelings toward the ethnic group and favoritism for the dominant group are the comments of an Asian American in the study: "If I could have chosen, I would choose to be American White, because it's America and I would then be in my country" (p. 44). Another Mexican American subject in the study agreed commenting that "I would choose to be White. They have more job opportunities and are more accepted" (p. 44).

Kim (1981) provides insight into the reasons behind the desire to join the dominant group during this period, having found similar feelings in the adult informants in her study. Her informants—10 Japanese American college students—recalled realizing their "differentness" from the White majority as children when they entered school. With this awareness came a period in childhood and adolescence when their self-concept began to change from positive or neutral to negative because they believed that being different carried a negative evaluation and that they themselves were responsible for their "differentness" and the lack of acceptance by the majority group.

The informants coped with this painful time by denying that differences—physical, cultural, and/or linguistic—existed between themselves and their peers while also denying their negative feelings toward themselves. Jared Matsunaga's comments exemplify this attempt at denial and the negative self-image associated with it (Tse, forthcoming). Although Jared excelled in school sports, was class president, and was voted most likely to succeed in high school, he had these feelings of insecurity:

"Secretly I hated myself, considered myself a coward for living in constant dread of being singled out on account of my race. Of course I always knew I'm Asian and that everyone else knew it too. It's just that I never acknowledged it, not even to members of my own family, and none of my schoolmates ever brought it up. My race was like some kind of bizarre open secret, though in my own mind I worried that it was a joke everyone shared at my expense" (p. 9).

Kim notes that this denial eventually leads to the informants identifying with the White majority group, and internalizing the dominant group's values and standards and seeing themselves through the eyes of White society. For many EMs, taking on dominant society standards meant judging themselves negatively when they did not "measure up." Andrea Kim, an Korean American journalist, described what she and her Asian peers did in high school to try to conform to White standards of beauty (Tse, forthcoming):

"I thought white people were very attractive. In fact I used to wish I had blue eyes and blond hair. In my high school, it was a fashionable thing for people to use Scotch tape, and make their eyes look more like whites. You can do it so that you make your lids have another fold. A lot of my friends in the summer would go to Japan because their families were there. They would have an operation to make their eyelids double. It was not an unusual thing. More people would dye their hair lighter—instead of black, they would make it brown" (p. 8-9).

The internalizing of White standards also translated in some EMs' desire to socialize and date outside of the ethnic American group and to disassociate themselves from the ethnic group altogether. This distancing took many forms. In terms of the heritage language, some EMs with proficiency in the language hid their ability in order to avoid being identified with the ethnic group. Maria Shao recounted how her knowledge of Chinese was a source of shame. She recalled that when she was in elementary school, "if I had friends over, I purposely spoke English to my parents. Normally, we only spoke Chinese at home. Because of the presence of a non-Chinese, I used to purposely speak English" (Tse, forthcoming, p. 12). Others who had little or no proficiency in the HL noted that they had no interest in learning the language because they feared that the ability to speak the language would mark them as a member of the undesirable ethnic group. At the same time, EMs emphasize their ability to speak English as a symbol of their majority group association. David Mura noted these feelings as a child: "I certainly didn't want to be thought of as Japanese American. I was American, pure and simple. I was proud I didn't know Japanese, that English was my sole tongue" (Tse, in press-b, p. 3).

Kim and others have noted that this is a painful time for EMs, a time when they desperately want to fit into the mainstream group, but feel that they fall short of the group's standards and may also face some level of rejection from the White group. At the same time, some of the EMs in these studies reject the ethnic group and view association with it as undesirable, considering it the reason for their alienation. In many ways, this leaves EMs in the position of having no group in which they belong and feel accepted.

Possibilities for Heritage Language Acquisition

Since stage 2 is a time of either ambivalent or negative feelings toward the ethnic group, EMs are more likely to prefer the majority group language than the heritage language. Therefore, in this stage, EMs may receive CI but may not achieve the CM necessary for high levels of HL development. Consider the following:

	CI	CM		HL Acquisition
Case 1	Yes	No	→	Unlikely
Case 2	No	No	→	Unlikely

EMs in this stage are highly unlikely to feel any sense of membership with the heritage language group, and therefore are not disposed to developing the HL.

It is not difficult to find EMs who receive no CI during this period. Some are raised in non-HL homes and communities; others, like Victor Merina, have HL-speaking parents but because of their fear that the children will not develop native English accents, decide against exposing the children to the HL (Tse, forthcoming) (Case 2). These EMs received no CI, and as a result, developed no proficiency in the language. Others who are exposed to the HL either in the home or in community language schools may acquire some HL ability, but not reach the levels they would otherwise attain if they had the desire to be a member of the HL "club." Without identification with the language group, EMs—even in HL-rich enviroments—may avoid contact with the language to whatever extent possible, such as forgoing HL-speaking friends or participation in HL-speaking activities, both of which would provide additional sources of CI (Case 1).

It is possible that the way in which CI is provided during this period determines whether the HL is developed. That is, if the CI is provided in a way that promotes CM, then acquisition is more likely to take place. Input from parents, for example, may not promote membership with the language group in the same way that peer input may. CI provided in mainstream schools and by HL-speaking peers may help the EM develop a positive attitude toward association with the HL group, thereby leading to more language acquisition.

STAGE 3: ETHNIC EMERGENCE

Nature of the Stage

In stage 2, EMs are uncomfortable with their ethnic association and yet are often unable to achieve full acceptance into the mainstream social group. It is in stage 3, Ethnic Emergence, that EMs face this paradox and confront the fact that they are uncomfortable with who they are and unclear about how they fit into the larger society. Entrance into stage 3 appears to occur gradually, though some critical events may accelerate movement into the stage.   Many move into Ethnic Emergence when they find themselves in settings where issues of ethnicity are more prominent and more openly addressed, such as in a university or a racially diverse city.

Individuals in Ethnic Emergence, having realized their inability to fully fit into and be accepted by mainstream society, confront their feelings of alienation and seek alternative groups to join. This period of exploration can be viewed as consisting of two steps: (a) awakening to one's own minority status, followed by (b) searching for an alternative group to join (Tse, in press-b).

EMs enter this period by facing the fact that they are members of an ethnic minority group. This "awakening" may be accompanied by a reexamination of their previous experiences and reinterpretation of interactions they have had with others. This was true for Karl Taro Greenfeld, who is of Japanese and Jewish descent. Karl recalled that as a child and teenager he felt socially integrated into the White community in which he was raised. Later, as an adult, he began to question whether he was truly accepted.

"I wonder whether I had intentionally not posited [sic] the racial slights directed at me. Looking back, I flash on scattered instances of blatant racism...[Those instances] were childish play, I know, but I remember the hurt and I remember hiding the pain. As a child I never wanted to show how these insults cut, because that would illuminate the difference between me and my playmates. And I always wanted to be like everyone else"(Tse, in press-b, p. 10-11).

Upon facing these types of experiences, some EMs become angry at the discrimination and differential treatment afforded to themselves and other ethnic minorities. Karl noted that "upon accepting that I was different and subject to a different set of standards than many of my acquaintances, my initial reaction was near-hysterical denunciation of anything that rubbed me the wrong way. I had gone from not noticing to always noticing discrimination" (p. 12). Because of feelings like these, many EMs become interested in discovering more about their ethnic heritage, and finding other ethnic groups in which they would have a better chance of finding acceptance, and by extension, more positive views of themselves.

Obvious groups EMs can turn to for possible membership are the ethnic group—the group associated with the home country—and the ethnic American group—for example, Chicanos and Asian Americans. To discover more about these groups, EMs may use a number of strategies. Phinney and Tarver (1988) reported that their African American adolescent subjects found out about their ethnic heritage by talking with family and friends about ethnic issues, reading books on the subject, and thinking about the effects of ethnicity on their lives. Phinney (1989) found similar types of exploration in her 64 U.S.-born African American, Asian American, and Latino tenth graders exemplified in the comments of one Mexican American subject: "I want to know what we do and how our culture is different from others. Going to festivals and cultural events helps me to learn more about my own culture and about myself" (p. 44). Other EMs socialize with ethnic or ethnic American peers and/or take trips to their ancestral homeland to build a connection to their ethnic heritage. Still others become interested in learning the heritage language. Many of these EMs regret not having learned the HL as children and believed that proficiency in the language would now help them gain acceptance into the ethnic homeland group.

Some in Ethnic Emergence embrace the ethnic culture to the extent of rejecting mainstream White culture, as was described in the study of Japanese Americans by Kim (1981). An informant in the study expressed it this way: "There was a point where my sister and I just fantasized about being just Japanese...I had swung a pendulum, I was literally so Asian American in thinking that my White friends that I had were accusing me of being ethnocentric" (p. 148). Another informant in the study changed her name to reflect her Japanese heritage and other informants wanted to associate exclusively with others of Asian descent. Overall, this stage is a period of confusion and even conflict as EMs experiment with various group associations and different "identities."

Possibilities for Heritage Language Acquisition

In contrast to stage 2 where EMs shy away from the HL, in Ethnic Emergence, many EMs become interested in exploring their ethnic heritage and heritage language. Therefore, stage 3 is an opportune time for EMs to acquire the HL, if CI is available.

	CI	CM		HL Acquisition
Case 1	Yes	Yes	→	Likely
Case 2	No	Yes	→	Unlikely

Writer David Mura, who chronicled his trip to his ethnic homeland of Japan, had experiences with HL study that illustrates both of these possibilities (Tse, in press-b). Initially, David enrolled in a Japanese language course in which he had many difficulties and could not keep up because the course did not provide him with CI (Case 2). Later, when he was in Japan, he received instruction from a tutor who created comprehensible lessons. David noted that although the sessions would be conducted almost entirely in Japanese, he and his wife were able to comprehend them with little difficulty, primarily because they centered around topics of interest to them both (Case 1). David noted that "often we found ourselves discussing things that had little to do with the lessons in our books," such as how Susie, David's wife, should handle men pinching her on the crowded trains or other personally relevant issues. As a result, David recalled developing the ability to hold extended conversations in Japanese and was amazed at "how rapidly we [he and his wife] progressed" (p. 16-17).

STAGE 4: ETHNIC IDENTITY INCORPORATION

Nature of the Stage

The final documented stage of ethnic identity development is Ethnic Identity Incorporation, where EMs find membership in the ethnic American group and resolve many of the conflicting feelings about their ethnic identity. Although nearly all of the available studies focus on adolescents or young adults who may not have reached this point in the process, there is some evidence of this stage. In general, EMs enter stage 4 after a relatively extended period of identity exploration and search. In the previous stage, some EMs believe that they have found satisfactory group membership in the ethnic homeland group, only to realize that they do not belong in that group either. This realization may come about as a result of members of the ethnic homeland group rejecting the EMs' membership and/or when the EMs come to see that that group no more incorporates their ethnic American experiences than the mainstream American group.

At this point, many begin to see that there is a possible third group to join: The ethnic American group made up of members who have gone through a similar ethnic identity search and who share, at least to some extent, the EMs' own experiences as an ethnic minority American. As one Chinese American informant noted, this discovery opened up a new world of possibilities. Stephanie Hom wrote:

"As I continue to learn about my cultural heritage and our place in white America I am discovering an entirely new world unknown to me before. There are people out there, Asian American writers, community leaders, actors and actresses who are addressing me in a language I can understand"(Tse, in press-b, p. 23).

EMs have also mentioned that discovering the ethnic American group changed their definition of what being American meant. Another informant, Keane Oka, put it this way. "You don't have to give up your cultural heritage or racial characteristics to become an 'American.' Just because I am a Japanese American, that doesn't mean that I am not an American. I am an American. But my Japanese heritage is my own, and I don't have to give it up"(p. 22). For these EMs, discovering the ethnic American group expanded their definition of mainstream culture, thereby making a place for themselves in broader society.

EMs in Ethnic Identity Incorporation note that this was a period of conflict resolution and an end to their previous feelings of alienation. As Kim (1981) observed in her informants, passing through this stage resulted in them "feeling better about themselves, boosting self-confidence and enhancing self-esteem" (p. 145) as they become proud to be an ethnic minority American and come to feel "at home with themselves" (p. 150).

Possibilities For Heritage Language Acquisition

In stage 4, the important factor that determines HL development is whether HL proficiency is valued in the ethnic minority American group in which the EM finds membership. If the HL is seen as important for membership, then the EM is likely to value it and want to acquire it. Therefore, there are four possibilities in stage 4:

	CI	CM[1]		HL Acquisition
Case 1	No	No	⟶	Unlikely
Case 2	No	Yes	⟶	Unlikely
Case 3	Yes	No	⟶	Unlikely
Case 4	Yes	Yes	⟶	Likely

[1]with a group that values the HL.

Again, whether EMs try to develop the HL in stage 4 depends on whether CI exists and whether they join a group that appreciates the language.

Previously mentioned informants Lara and Keith provide clear cases of two of the possibilities (Tse, in press-a). In this stage, Lara found membership in a Filipino group that she believes requires proficiency in Tagalog and continues to be interested in developing her ability in the language (Case 3). Keith, on the other hand, joined an Asian American group that does not require Chinese proficiency, and although he has positive attitudes toward the language, has no plans to acquire it (Case 1).

An EM in the Case 2 situation may have a desire to acquire the language but may not have access to the heritage language in the form of language courses or have entre into an immigrant community. Those who fall under the Case 4 scenario have both a desire to acquire the language and the access to language input. An EM in this situation may have found opportunities for language study, socializing with HL speakers, travel abroad, or other methods to obtain CI.

Conclusion

Considering the possibilities for heritage language development, it is more likely that HL acquisition will occur when an EM is not in stage 2, CI is available, and membership is found in a group that values the HL. Very little is known about how to promote group membership, but we do know that people join groups that they see as desirable. Providing EM students with information on and/or exposure to their heritage and ethnic minority American groups may help them find connections to the culture and feel more favorably toward the group and its members.

Unlike group membership, we know much more about how to provide comprehensible input to language learners. HL acquirers with very little or no proficiency in the language are likely to benefit from interesting comprehension-based lessons taught in low anxiety settings (Krashen and Terrell, 1983). Those with higher proficiency can be encouraged to read for pleasure, which has been found to be highly effective in language acquisition (Krashen, 1993; McQuillan, 1996). Several researchers have documented the effects of using pleasure reading or "free voluntary reading" in the HL classroom, finding that such programs are very successful in promoting language acquisition (reviewed in McQuillan, this volume).

The ethnic identity development process discussed in this paper represents the experiences of a growing segment of American society—a population of minority Americans who have achieved some level of assimilation into mainstream society. As I mentioned above, this model was not intended to describe the experiences of all minority Americans but was developed to represent the experiences of ethnic minorities described in an emerging literature. Developing a better understanding of the stages that EM children, adolescents, and adults may go through could help counselors provide support services for these students and aid language educators to better formulate programs for heritage language acquisition.

Note

1. This model of ethnic identity development may also apply to nonracial minorities if their EM status emerges as an important issue in their lives. However, some EMs who belong to the racial majority may never suffer the consequences of ethnic minority status and may never go through the four stages described here.

References

Giles, H., and Byrne, J.L. (1982) "An intergroup approach to second language acquisition." *Journal of Multilingual and Multicultural Development* **3:** 17–24.

Kim, J. (1981) "Processes of Asian American identity development: A study of Japanese American women's perceptions of their struggle to achieve positive identities as Americans of Asian ancestry" (Doctoral dissertation, University of Massachusetts, 1981). *Dissertation Abstracts International*, 42, 1551.

Krashen, S. (1985) *The Input Hypothesis: Issues and Implications.* Beverly Hills: Laredo.

Krashen, S. (1993) *The Power of Reading.* Englewood, CO: Libraries Unlimited.

Krashen, S., and Terrell, T.D. (1983) *The Natural Approach: Language Acquisition in the Classroom.* New York: Prentice Hall.

McQuillan, J. (1996) "How should heritage languages be taught? The effects of a free voluntary reading program." *Foreign Language Annals* **29(1):** 56–72.

Phinney, J.S. (1989) "Stages of ethnic identity in minority group adolescents." *Journal of Early Adolescence* **9:** 34–49.

Phinney, J.S., and Tarver, S. (1988) "Ethnic identity search and commitment in Black and White eighth graders." *Journal of Early Adolescence* **8(3):** 265–277.

Tse, L. (1996) "The effects of ethnic identity formation on attitudes toward native language development." Paper presented at the Annual Meeting of the American Education Research Association, New York.

Tse, L. "The effects of ethnic identity formation on language attitudes: Evidence for a developmental model." In the 1996 National Association of Asian Pacific Education Conference Proceedings. Oakland, CA: NAAPAE. In press (a).

Tse, L. "Finding a place to be: Asian Americans in ethnic identity exploration." *Adolescence.* In press (b).

Tse, L. "The effects of Ethnic Ambivalence/Evasion on heritage language attitudes: An analysis of Asian American narratives." Forthcoming.

3. The Negative Consequences of Heritage Language Loss and Why We Should Care

Grace Cho and Stephen Krashen

"What happens to familial relations when the language children give up happens to be the only language that parents speak? What is lost when children and parents cannot communicate easily to one another? (Wong-Fillmore, 1991, pp. 342-343)

"I can't even hold an ordinary conversation with my parents." (Sandy)

Contrary to popular opinion, immigrants to the United States are acquiring English rapidly (Krashen, 1996); also contrary to popular opinion, they are also losing their family or "heritage" languages rapidly.

Educational researchers have long recognized that maintaining the heritage language is not an additional burden; bilinguals do as well as or better than monolinguals in society. In addition, there is no evidence that multilingualism is bad for society. There is, thus, no evidence that bilingualism is harmful; in fact, it appears to be beneficial (Krashen, this volume).

Is there, however, any reason to be overly concerned when heritage languages are lost? The research (Krashen, this volume) showing that bilingualism is not harmful and is perhaps beneficial suggests that bilingualism is desirable, but it is a luxury. Recent observations show, however, that there are strong reasons to maintain the heritage language.

Wong-Fillmore (1991) describes two cases of intergenerational conflict in which heritage language loss played a role. In one case, children received corporal punishment for showing disrespect for their grandfather who was visiting from Korea. The children in the family had stopped speaking Korean at home, and they made errors using markers that marked respect when trying to speak Korean to their grandfather. This linguistic error was interpreted as disrespect.

In a second case, a mother and her 17-year-old son actually came to blows "when words failed them" (p. 344). The mother spoke only Spanish and her children refused to use Spanish, and even "do not acknowledge it when their parents speak it" (p. 344).

In this paper, we present cases confirming that Wong-Fillmore's observations are valid. The cases we present also show that the problem extends beyond parent-child and grandparent-child communication; lack of heritage language competence affects communication with a much wider social group.

This data comes from two sources:

(1) Informal interviews were conducted with twelve Korean American university students or recent college graduates who work in American companies in California. All interviews were in English and each lasted about one hour. Questions were asked about language use in the family, attitudes toward the heritage language, and experiences using the HL outside the family. All of the subjects were either born in the US or came to the US before school age, and reported that they spoke Korean fluently before elementary school, and all say they are now more comfortable speaking English. All use English with their siblings and friends. Subjects were contacted through various Korean language classes, a Korean church, and through personal acquaintances. Six of the 12 were currently enrolled in a heritage language Korean class.

(2) Sixty Korean American students enrolled in Korean heritage language classes at the University of Southern California and at a private language school in Los Angeles at the time of this study filled out a survey in which they were asked about their reasons for studying their heritage language and conflicts and communication problems they had had with their heritage language. Most were born in the US. Of those who were not, most came to the US at age eight or earlier.

We first present examples of individual subjects' comments about their problems, then briefly summarize the data for the entire group. We present our most important result first: Nearly all of our subjects reported problems communicating in Korean. The exceptions had unusual sources of input. Su Mi (real names not used) maintained and developed her Korean by brokering (interpreting) for her parents; Emily lived alone with her monolingual Korean-speaking grandmother for many years; Susan always lived in a community with many Korean speakers, went to a Korean school on weekends, and participated in activities involving Korean culture; Elena held several jobs which helped her develop her Korean.

Intergenerational Conflict

Several subjects confirmed that their loss of their ability to use the heritage language interfered with their ability to communicate with their parents. Very ordinary communication was possible, but children were not able to communicate more subtle thoughts to their parents.

Sandy expressed it this way: "My parents and I do have a communication gap, a communication problem. Not in just a sophisticated way. I can't even hold a normal conversation with my parents. I just say my thoughts once and I repeat it constantly until they understand."

Another subject, Cami, noted: "I can say the most subtle thing to my friends and they understand the whole color of it. But, with my parents, I have to literally say everything like, 'I am sad! ... This is why ...'. However, with my friends I just talk about all different aspects of how I am sad and how it reminds me of the time ... and how I can get over it with what I have learned. But with my parents, I am just reporting to them. It totally loses the interactive connection .... ."

Su Mi is able to speak to her parents in Korean, but her younger sister has problems communicating: "I see barriers between my mom and my sister. I can explain what I want ... like when my sister wants something, if she says it directly to my mom, my mom just doesn't get it, and they get frustrated with each other and they are like fighting, tension ... I can just say 'Mom, this is what she meant and my mom says 'Oh, why doesn't she say so ... okay ... go to the movie'."

Justin reports that "when speaking with my parents, sometimes I am unable to communicate ... I have a language deficiency. Many arguments and explanations are cut short because I lack the language ability."

Christine feels that her Korean is "pretty good," but says that "It's hard to open up my emotions with my parents, so we always have to use symbols, body language ...."

Rosa reported that "due to my lack of vocabulary in Korean, I tend to have a difficult time communicating with my parents. Sometimes it results in unnecessary arguments which could have been resolved quickly. It also makes me feel bad when I can't talk to my grandmother or tell her things ...."

Finally, Erika said that "it is frustrating when I'm speaking with my parents and we can't fully comprehend what we're trying to say to each other. I hate it when I eat dinner with my parents and they always carry on their own conversation that I can only half understand. Yet, they complain that we don't eat as a family enough. I hate having something to say but not being able to say it."

In a Los Angeles Times report, Kang (1996) found a similar pattern: "Communication is difficult because they (parents) lack a common language with which they and their children can express themselves fluently." One parent said that she wished there was a simultaneous interpreter when she talked to her children (p. A12).

Interactions with the HL Community

Loss of the heritage language also interferes with interactions outside the immediate family. Some subjects reported a feeling of isolation and exclusion from members of their own ethnic group. Sandy and Cami commented on problems with family acquaintances and people in the neighborhood where the heritage language is spoken:

Sandy: "Whenever someone calls my home and they don't speak English, the only word I say is my parents went to 'market' in Korean. That's all. After that, if they ask me anything else I get so frustrated. I wish I could be very personable and ask about their kids ... because many times I know who they are."

Cami: "I wish I could interact better. With American merchants, we joke around, but when we come to a Korean store ... I feel bad that I can't speak in Korean. Think of an interaction we do in a store in English, joking around ... but, the only thing I could say is 'Thank you.' It's unfortunate! It's hard enough for them already to deal with others who don't speak Korean and I don't want them to feel animosity toward me. I feel like we are robbing the Korean community of our wonderful resources ... too bad we can't communicate."

Kris reported the following incident: "Once I went to Koreatown to get a hair cut to get ready for a sorority event. The hair dresser started doing a French braid, but I asked her to do a French twist. I kept saying 'no, no.' The two people with me were Filipino and Japanese. The hair dressers were talking about us. You know, once they knew that you didn't speak Korean fluently, they were saying to each other that we were 'Chinese, Japanese' ... it was kind of an insult for me ...."

Kris also related that "If I go to Koreatown or go to a Korean restaurant, usually I would say 'an young ha sae yo,' meaning 'how are you?' and they think I speak Korean fluently ... it's kind of embarrassing that I can't speak my own language."

Vicky reported that "I have many problems speaking with relatives and friends of my parents. It's quite frustrating because I am not able to say what I want."

Carol feels "separated from other Koreans because they mostly speak Korean to each other and even at church ...."

Sandy works in a company that employs a number of fluent Korean speakers: "In my office, my coworkers and the board decided it was a good idea to get all Koreans together to network and get to know each other. All these people spoke Korean as their first language ... but the fact that they had to sit there putting so much effort to speak English just so that I could understand them ... made me feel so awkward and frustrated at that point I decided to not hang around with them, it was too much of a headache for everyone."

Julian said that "last summer I worked at Asian Airlines and the experience as a whole was good. However, because of my limited ability to speak, peope would joke about my accent and lack of vocabulary."

Irlene, now enrolled in a class to improve her Korean, is there because "there are people ... important to me that I want to communicate with ... my family, parents, relatives, community people ... that's the reason I took Korean." She wishes she could read the Korean newspaper "because it will make me more aware of what kinds of news my parents get and to be more aware of their perceptions."

Sonia reported that "At home, when we have company, I feel left out because my communication skills are limited and I guess the people get fed up with me, too. After a while, they just ignore me since I can't speak Korean that well and they don't really speak English."

Garreton (1995) provides additional data. One of her subjects, Carol, a Korean-American college freshman, has studied Korean seriously, and noted that others are interested in doing so:

> I know of a couple of older people who are trying to go back to school now [to study Korean] ... they feel like they've lost a lot of things in their younger years, that they couldn't go back to. My cousin is in her thirties, and she scrambled to get back into classes. She had to find a class so she could learn [Korean] now because she feels that she is almost isolated from the family at family functions. Everyone speaks Korean, and she just kind of sits there and says "yes" or "hi" and I see that in my parents' friends' children. A lot of the older ones are desperately trying to get into Korean now because they want to be in the family, they want to have interaction with the family.

Using the Heritage Language with Speakers Outside the US

Those who have lost even some ability in the heritage language, or who have not developed high levels of competence, face special problems when visiting the country where the language is spoken, especially when they look like native speakers. Garreton's subject, Christine, discussed her experience in Japan:

> The Japanese would give me a hard time because all my friends were Caucasian and even though I spoke much better Japanese than they did, I wasn't up to par with the Japanese natives of my age, so they thought I was really strange, if not dumb.

When Sue visited her relatives in Korea, her cousins ridiculed her, calling her "an American girl" because of her lack of knowledge of the Korean language.

Cami had tremendous difficulties when her aunt called from Korea: "She never spoke to me before and we only exchanged three sentences and her final words were: 'Why don't you learn to speak Korean?'"

Summary

Table 1 summarizes complete results, dividing the subjects into two groups: those who were surveyed and those who were interviewed in depth.

Table 1
Summary of Problems with Heritage Language

Subjects	n	Family & Relatives	Korean Community	Other	No Conflicts
Survey	60	32	43	3	6
Interview	12	9	9	2	4

One would expect that those enrolled in a heritage language course would report problems with their heritage language, and this is what was found; every heritage language student reported problems. Of the six interviewed subjects not enrolled in classes, however, several reported problems (e.g. Cami and Sandy).

Discussion

The general public is under the impression that immigrants and their children hold on to their family languages and resist acquiring English. In reality, English is acquired surprisingly rapidly and family languages are being lost (Krashen, 1996). The subjects interviewed in this study confirm that this is the case, and consistently report that their inadequacies in the heritage language cause problems and discomfort for them.

Although the study dealt with a small number of subjects, and they were a sample of convenience, the consistency of the results suggests that these problems are widespread. Our interviewees had similar backgrounds: All spoke the heritage language well as a small child, and most reported at least some difficulties.

Is the solution simply to provide more heritage language development in school? One can also ask whether this situation is something that educational systems should be concerned with; should we simply insist that all parents acquire English to very high levels of competence?

Our view is that heritage language development in school is desirable and important.

First, the ability to communicate comfortably with family and other members of the community is not the only advantage of heritage language development, as noted in the introduction to this paper. Bilingualism provides cognitive and practical benefits.

Second, heritage language education can be considered much more than simply a service to help children speak their heritage language better; heritage language education is also multicultural education, with the goal of helping students understand cultural universals and the commonalities that unite people.

Thus, even if one accepts the argument that school should not concern itself with family problems, there are strong, independent reasons for heritage language development.

Third, parents are not always in a position to acquire high levels of English competence. The drive to acquire English is powerful and many immigrant parents have acquired English; Kris, for example, noted that "we can communicate in English so we don't have any language problem. Sometimes we do get a little off, but we don't have a problem." Most immigrants who have not, however, simply have not had the chance. Cami's father told her that he had not acquired English because he had been "too busy." Not everyone has the time and opportunity to enroll in ESL classes.

Finally, we believe that ensuring strong parent-child communication is an excellent investment for both the individual and the society. Without it, children loose a great deal. As Wong-Fillmore notes:

> What is lost is no less than the means by which parents socialize their children: When parents are unable to talk to their children, they cannot easily convey to them their values, beliefs, understanding, or wisdom about how to cope with their experiences. They cannot teach them about the meaning of work, or about personal responsibility, or what it means to be a moral or ethical person in a world with too many choices and too few guideposts to follow. What is lost are the bits of advice, the consejos [advice] parents should be able to offer children in the everyday interactions with them. Talk is a crucial link between parents and children. (p. 343)

From our data we can add that what is lost is the means by which children gain wisdom and experience from other elders and the heritage language community as well.

References

Garreton, M. (1995) "Native speakers as language learners." In T. Dvork (Ed.), *Voices From the Field: Experiences and Beliefs of our Constituents.* Lincolnwood, IL: National Textbook Company.

Kang, K.C. (1996) "Korean Americans dream of crimson." *Los Angeles Times*, September 25, 1996, A1, A12.

Krashen, S. (1996) *Under Attack: The Case Against Bilingual Education.* Culver City: Language Education Associates.

Wong Fillmore, L. (1991) "When learning a second language means losing the first." *Early Childhood Research Quarterly* **6:** 323–346.

4. Language Shyness and Heritage Language Development

Stephen Krashen

Heritage languages (HL) are languages spoken in the family, but not in the dominant society. HL's are difficult to maintain, let alone develop; shift to the dominant language of the country is very rapid, and is generally complete in a few generations (Veltman, 1983; Krashen, 1996). In this paper, we discuss one possible cause for the loss of heritage languages, a phenomena that appears to be quite common but has not been described in the professional literature. It is a kind of "language shyness" particular to speakers of heritage languages. It occurs when an HL speaker knows the HL fairly well, but not perfectly. What is often lacking are late-acquired aspects of language, aspects that typically do not interfere with communication but are important politeness or social class markers.

Because HL speakers are members of the HL group, their imperfections are very salient to more proficient speakers, who may respond by correcting and even with ridicule. Such responses can be devastating to less proficient HL speakers. Error correction and criticism do not help them; they have the opposite effect: Rather than risk error, they interact less in the HL. This sets up a vicious cycle—less interaction means less input, and less input means less proficiency. Because language is such a clear marker of social group membership, it could also contribute to alienation from the HL group.

The case histories presented here do not demonstrate how widespread the problem is, but they do demonstrate that it exists. My suspicion, after discussing this phenomena with many HL speakers, is that this kind of shyness is not infrequent. (Cases A, B, and C were students of mine in a graduate language education class.)

Case A: As a child in a city on the East Coast of the United States, A's parents spoke Spanish to her, and she feels that she acquired both Spanish and English at the same time, as her older sister preferred English:

> As I grew older, I began to use Spanish less ... I spent my time at school and with my friends who were all born in America. Like many children, school and friends were of more interest to me than my parents and therefore I purposely set out to speak more English. Notice that I say speak more English, not speak less Spanish. I never set out to leave my native language behind. However, I did just that for reasons not of my choosing.

> I began to realize as I spoke Spanish to my relatives, they would constantly correct my grammar or pronunciation. Of course, since I was a fairly young child the mistakes I made were "cute" to them and they would giggle and correct me. This ... would annoy me to no end. I wasn't trying to be "cute"; I was trying to be serious. My relatives would say, "You would never know that you are the daughter of an Argentine." Comments like these along with others are what I now believe shut me off to Spanish ....

Case B: B also grew up in a town in New Jersey that was 85% Hispanic. Both English and Spanish were spoken in her household. She was the youngest of five children, so "by the time I was born, there was a great deal of English spoken in the house." Her parents would speak to her in Spanish and she would answer in English:

> Growing up I was the butt of many jokes ... When I was nine years old ... a man called, speaking Spanish very quickly. I stumbled through the conversation and got his name, Jorge. I left the message for my father that simply read "HORHEAD CALLED." They laughed about that for weeks and still bring it up to this day.

> ... every laugh and giggle chipped away at my self-esteem ... the innocent jokes and cracks took their toll on me and began the creation of a barrier between myself and my family....

Unlike A, B lived in an environment where a great deal of the heritage language was used among her generation, which added to her problem:

> Along with family pressure, peer pressure played a large role as well ... my surrounding environment was filled with Spanish. Most of my

peers were fluent native speakers. There was an unspoken expecta-
tion that if you were Hispanic, you should be able to speak the language fluently. This pressure put up a barrier with my friends as well.

Tragically, B blamed herself for not speaking Spanish well:

> My self-esteem reached an all-time low in college. Several of my
> peers made well-meaning, but harsh comments upon hearing my
> Spanish. This was the final blow. It was then I made the decision that
> I wouldn't speak unless I could speak fluently, grammatically correct,
> and with a proper native accent. I couldn't even feel comfortable
> describing myself as bilingual on my resume. I had to add "limited
> proficiency" in parentheses to ease my conscience ... I was ashamed
> of being Puerto Rican and living in a bilingual home and never learn-
> ing Spanish ... the only conclusion I could come to was that it was
> somehow my fault ...

Case C: C, a student in a university level Spanish for native speaker
course recalls:

> My father still ... interrupts me repeatedly every time I speak Spanish
> in his presence to correct my grammar or pronunciation. I do my best
> to speak only English in his company ... As soon as the need for me
> to speak arises, I find everything I know, can write and read, coming
> out in the wrong order, and the vocabulary I know suddenly becomes
> extremely limited and elementary. This occurs most often around
> those individuals who are native speakers.

Experiences in Foreign Language Classes

HL speakers are often quite successful in foreign language classes; they
are, after all, "false beginners" (or false intermediates). But not all HL
speakers succeed in foreign language classes. Often, classes focus on
conscious learning of grammatical rules that are late acquired. Some
HL speakers may not have learned or acquired these items. It can happen that non-speakers of the HL who are good at grammar will out-
perform HL speakers on grammar tests and get higher grades in the
language class, even though the non-speaker of the HL may be inca-
pable of communicating the simplest idea in the language, while the
HL speaker may be fairly competent in everyday conversation. This
only adds to the HL speakers' problem, giving them even less confidence in their command of the HL.

There is some empirical evidence supporting this conjecture. Kataoka (1978) compared Japanese American students with non Japanese American students taking Japanese language courses at the university level. The groups had similar GPA's and grades in Japanese classes, but the non-Japanese students devoted significantly more time to the study of Japanese, had significantly more interest in speaking Japanese, and had higher scores on a language aptitude test (aptitude for grammar study; Krashen, 1981).

The Japanese American students, however, had greater conversational fluency and reported more use of Japanese outside of class, but there was no difference between the groups in confidence in Japanese spoken proficiency. Teachers recognized that Japanese Americans were more fluent, but did not rank them more highly in accuracy and actually rated non-Japanese higher in writing. Clearly, teachers did not value the abilities the Japanese Americans had, and made their evaluations to

Table 1

Predictors of Grades in Japanese Class Among Japanese American Students

CLASS GRADE AND	
length of residence in Japan	.13
use of Japanese at home	.05
parents speak Japanese	.07

from: Kataoka (1978)

a significant extent on the basis of late-acquired aspects of language that are taught directly and emphasized in traditional language classes. The fact that HL speakers were more fluent but did not have greater confidence in their spoken proficiency suggests that the Japanese American students internalized their teachers' judgments.

Katoka reported low correlations between comprehensible input-related variables and grades (table 1), confirming that spoken fluency and class success are not strongly related.

If HL speakers do well in a class, there is no victory: After all, they are members of the HL group and are expected to speak the language. HL speakers are thus in a no-win situation in such a language class, even if they get high grades.

A's case exemplifies the problem: Her background with Spanish did not make high school Spanish a snap. The emphasis was on learning, not acquisition:

Classmates' voices from high school keep ringing in my head. "What are you taking Spanish classes for? They must be easy for you. Oh, you're taking it for an easy 'A', aren't you?" ... Truthfully, the Spanish classes I took in high school were hard and I had to•work with my grammar and accent for long periods of time.

Instructors, like other more proficient HL speakers, often have very high expectations for HL speaking students. C recalls:

... the most intimidating and painful experiences I have had ... while attempting to learn Spanish have been dealt me by native Spanish speaking instructors ... at the university ... It is a subject of discussion among many students, native Spanish speakers as well as native English speakers that these professors, but certainly not all, are particularly hard and much more demanding of students who are of Latino background ....

Those with no knowledge of the HL face special problems in regular foreign language classes. Robert, described in Romo and Falbo (1996), came from a Mexican American family in Austin but did not speak Spanish:

His parents did not speak Spanish at home. They encouraged Robert, however, to study Spanish in high school. Robert said that he felt uncomfortable in class:

" ... I don't like volunteering there ... She gets mad at me. They expect me to volunteer since I'm Mexican, but I don't do it. The teacher gets mad at me. There are only, like, two or three Mexicans in there. I told them, 'You know, if I knew Spanish, why would I be taking the class?' "They always expect me to do things and I don't do it." (Romo and Falbo, p. 23)

Robert stopped taking Spanish classes after two years.

The Consequences of Language Shyness

As noted above, language shyness often leads to less competence, and even more shyness. The consequences are serious: The speaker may eventually give up on the HL. This means a loss of the economic and cognitive benefits of bilingualism, and can also result in estrangement from the HL community. Giving up on the HL can also affect "ethnic emergence," a stage many minority members go through in which there is increased interest in one's ethnic heritage. It may be that ethnic emergence is an important step toward attaining a positive self image and the acceptance of both cultures (Tse, this volume).

The Cure

The ideal cure for the weak HL speaker would be to change people's attitudes about correctness in language, to persuade stronger HL speakers not to ridicule or correct, but to tolerate weak HL speakers' errors, and to encourage interaction in the HL, a much better way to develop accurate HL competence. This is not likely to happen. Our standards for language are very high and feelings about correctness are strong (Finegan, 1980): Group membership requires perfection. In addition, many strong HL speakers' personal theories of language development are based on correction, not comprehensible input, despite the theoretical evidence against correction (Krashen, 1994).

Our usual prescription for the HL speaker are special classes (e.g. "Spanish for Native Speakers"). Such classes have been described in the professional literature but have never, to my knowledge, been evaluated. Moreover, from the published descriptions, it appears to be the case that nearly all such classes are based on traditional methodology, with direct teaching of grammar, reading comprehension and writing style. For those who are well educated in the HL, such classes are simply a test that they pass, because they will have already acquired most if not all of the material that is consciously taught. For weak HL speakers, such classes might only make their situation worse.

Table 2
Predictors of Confidence in Speaking Among Japanese American Students
(Kataoka, 1978)

CORRELATION WITH CONFIDENCE IN SPEAKING JAPANESE

Variables Reflecting Comprehensible Input	
length of residence in Japan	.38
use of Japanese at home	.29
parents speak Japanese	.29
Variables Reflecting Study	
length of study	.12
grade in class	.01

Kataoka reported that for Japanese American students in Japanese classes (see above), correlations between confidence in speaking and length of study and success in study were very low, but correlations between confidence in speaking and variables reflecting comprehensible input were higher (table 2). This suggests that the solution may be heritage language classes that provide comprehensible input, comprehensible input that some HL acquirers find difficult to obtain in the informal environment.

An especially powerful form of comprehensible input is free voluntary reading, an activity that can build language competence tremendously but can be done in private (ideal for shy heritage language speakers). One way of helping HL students establish a reading habit in the HL is to teach popular literature. In McQuillan (1996), twenty HL speakers participated in a ten week class that was focused on free reading, literature circles (small group discussion of what was read) and a survey of popular literature. There was no direct teaching of vocabulary or any other aspect of language. Sixteen of the 20 increased their score on a vocabulary test, with only the highest-scoring pretest students not showing gains. Such results are consistent with a vast number of studies showing that pleasure reading is an excellent way of developing advanced competence in language.

McQuillan (personal communication) provides a case history that supports the idea that reading is helpful for HL development:

> GS was a student in my class who grew up in the United States with Spanish-speaking parents. As an English-dominant speaker, he felt very insecure about his Spanish, but felt it was important to learn how to speak it well. He enrolled in a Spanish for native speakers course in high school, which he found "very hard," getting a grade of B-. He did not continue to read or have much contact with Spanish after the course, however, probably because the focus of the course was on grammar and "literature."
>
> When he enrolled in the Spanish for native speakers course in the university, he had still never read an entire book in Spanish, but was eager to learn. Having been given the choice of readings for the class, he began to read the sports page of the local Spanish newspaper, and pick up books in Spanish from the local library. He joined the campus Mexican American club and was considering studying in Mexico over the summer. His confidence in using Spanish had clearly increased as a result of the exposure to the pleasure reading and cultural themes in the classroom.

Such classes can be supplemented with subject matter teaching in the HL, with an emphasis on cultural material (e.g. history, current events) that will make students' reading more comprehensible and that will contribute additionally to HL competence.

There is mounting evidence that heritage language development is not only harmless, it is also beneficial (Tienda and Neidert, 1984; Fernandez and Nielson, 1986; Tienda and Neidert, 1986). HL development has practical and cognitive advantages and also helps heritage language speakers interact with and learn from their elders and community (Wong-Fillmore, 1991). Heritage language development appears to be a good investment for the individual as well as for our society.

References

Fernandez, R. and Neilsen, F. (1986) "Bilingualism and Hispanic scholastic achievement: Some baseline results." *Social Science Research* **15:** 43–70.

Finegan, E. (1980) *Attitudes toward English Usage: The History of a War of Words.* New York: Teachers College Press, Columbia University.

Kataoka, H. (1978) "Motivations and Attitudes of Japanese-American students toward Learning the Japanese Language." Ph.D. dissertation, University of Illinois, School of Education.

Krashen, S. (1981) *Second Language Acquisition and Second Language Learning.* New York: Prentice Hall.

Krashen, S. (1994) "The input hypothesis and its rivals." In N. Ellis (Ed.), *Implicit and Explicit Learning of Languages.* London: Academic Press. pp. 45–77.

Krashen, S. (1996) *Under Attack: The Case Against Bilingual Education.* Culver City, CA: Language Education Associates.

McQuillan, J. (1996) "How should heritage languages be taught? The effects of a free voluntary reading program." *Foreign Language Annals* **29 (1):** 56–72.

Nielsen, F. and Lerner, S,. (1986) "Language skills and school achievement of bilingual Hispanics." *Social Science Research* **15:** 209–240.

Tienda, M. and Niedert, L. (1984) "Language, education, and the socioeconomic achievement of Hispanic origin men." *Social Science Quarterly* **65**: 519–536.

Veltman, C. (1983) *Language Shift in the United States*. Berlin: Mouton.
Wong-Fillmore, L. (1991) "When learning a second language means losing the first." *Early Childhood Research Quarterly* **6**: 323–346.

5. Affecting Affect: The Impact of Heritage Language Programs on Student Attitudes[1]

Lucy Tse

Heritage language (HL) programs have a long tradition in North American education, dating back to the earliest days of its history (Crawford, 1991). Little was known, however, about the effects of heritage language instruction and of bilingualism in general until the early parts of this century when attention began to be focused on their cognitive and linguistic effects. Despite this research, relatively little effort has been devoted to examining the effects of heritage language development on affective factors, such as language attitudes and ethnic group opinions. The purpose of this chapter is to review the existing studies on the relationship between school-sponsored heritage language programs and attitudinal factors in order to identify gaps in the literature and to suggest directions for future research. The available studies on the effects of HL programs on affect will be examined under three general categories: 1) heritage language attitudes, 2) ethnic group attitudes, and 3) students' views of themselves.

Affect and Language Acquisition

Although there has been no previous synthesis of research on heritage language exposure and affect, attitudinal factors have been found to be important in language acquisition. Gardner and Lambert proposed two types of attitudinal orientation to acquiring a language. An "instrumental" orientation refers to "a desire to gain social recognition or economic advantages through knowledge of a foreign language," while an "integrative" orientation is a "desire to be like representative members of the other language community" (Gardner and Lambert, 1972, p. 14).

Krashen (1981) suggests that while both integrative and instrumental orientations will motivate language acquisition, those integratively oriented are more likely to acquire those parts of language that facilitate integration into a group, beyond that needed for strict communication. Further, these attitudinal orientations affect language acquisition by determining to a large extent the amount of interaction the acquirer has with members of the target language community. As the desire to join the language group drives the integratively motivated learner, he/she is more likely to seek social contact. The more the interaction, the more comprehensible input the acquirer is likely to be exposed to and to acquire. For this reason, attitudinal factors act as barriers or bridges to new language input, the "essential environmental ingredient" for language acquisition (Krashen, 1985, p. 2).

Studies examining the impact of integrative and instrumental attitudes on language acquisition show that students who are integratively oriented are generally more successful in acquiring a language than those who are instrumentally motivated (Gardner, 1985). Consistent with these findings is Giles and Byrne's (1982) proposition that language acquisition is dependent upon an individual's perceived membership in a target language group. As Tajfel (1974) points out, individuals make sense of the world by creating social categories, and our self-concept is determined by the groups we believe we have membership in and the comparisons we make between groups. For a favorable self-concept to result, individuals must perceive that comparisons between their own groups and other social/ethnic groups are in their own favor.

In terms of heritage language acquisition, language plays an important role as one of the most salient ethnic group identifiers (Taylor, Bassili, and Aboud, 1973; Giles, Taylor, and Bourhis, 1977), and as a likely social group marker used for those social comparisons. For this reason, language acquisition is facilitated when an individual has positive attitudes toward the language, feels positively about the ethnic group in which he or she is a member, and ultimately feels that these associations result in an overall satisfactory self-evaluation (Tse, forthcoming). In the following section, the impact of heritage language programs on these three dimensions will be discussed.

Effects of Heritage Language Programs on Student Affect

ORGANIZATION OF STUDIES

Studies are discussed below under three general headings: language attitudes, ethnic group attitudes, and views of oneself. As can be seen in Table 1, a majority of the studies report on more than one outcome, and therefore, need to be discussed under more than one heading. For the sake of brevity, general descriptions of the study will only be included with the study's first mention.

DEFINITION OF KEY TERMS

Several key terms used in this review require definition. The term "heritage language (HL) programs" is broadly defined as those sponsored by public or private schools that use the language and/or promote its acquisition. The term includes the various forms of bilingual education, heritage language supplemental schools (sometimes referred to as "ethnic schools," "after-school schools," or "Saturday schools"), short-term intervention language programs, and travel abroad programs. Although the purpose for establishing these programs may differ widely, common among them is the intention to develop student proficiency in the heritage language for its own sake, to aid in second language (L2) acquisition, and/or to assist general learning.

The three categories of outcomes—language attitudes, ethnic group attitudes, and self-evaluation—are defined as follows: "Language attitude" refers to any affective factors related to language, including language study and one's own language ability, and "ethnic group attitudes" is defined as attitudinal outcomes relating to an individual's ethnic/language minority group and/or other ethnic/language groups. The third category, "self-evaluation," relates to attitudes toward oneself, including self-esteem, confidence, feelings of belonging, and personal power.

Table 1

Effects of HL Programs on Affect: A Summary of Studies

Study	Sample	Treatment	Results
Effects on Language and Attitudes			
Feuerverger (1989)	n=112 grade 8 Italian Canandians	integrated vs after school	Integrated group had more positive attitudes toward HL
Feuerverger (1994)	Low SES Elementary School	HL books added to school library	greater appreciation of HL
Garrett, Griffiths, James & Scholfield (1994)	n=56 age 10 & 11 Welsh or Punjabi dominant children	prewriting activities in HL or English over 12 weeks	no difference in attitudes toward English, HL or bilingualism
Lambert & Cazabon (1994)	n=57 grades 4-6 English & Spanish native speakers	2-way bilingual education, at least 4 years	Majority report confidence using both languages, wish to continue acquiring Spanish
Lambert, Giles, & Picard (1975)	n=68 age 10 French Americans	4 yrs of bilingual ed vs. none	Bilingual ed: Upper class French rated over English, aspire to middle class French Canandian group; No bil. ed: English rated over French, aspire to English speaking group.
Muller, Penner, Blowers, Jones & Mosychuk (1976)	n=70 grade 1 Ukranian Americans	bilingual ed. vs. no bil. ed	Bil ed. English proficiency as good as all-English; 80% liked doing school work in Ukranian; Prof. in Ukranian better

Study	Sample	Treatment	Results
Xidis (1993)	n=139 grade 7&8 Greek Americans	Greek schools vs. all English	Greek schools: More positive attitude toward HL
Effect on Attitudes toward Ethnic Group			
Blake, Lambert, Sidoti & Wolfe (1981)	n=360 grade 6,11 Canadians, monolingual English and French, bilingual	comparison of all-English all-French, French immersion	Bilinguals made friends more with children of other ethnic groups earlier in life; Imm. students view French and English Canadians as more similar to each other
Feuerverger (1989)	see above	see above	Integrated group had higher ethnolinguistic vitality
Feuerverger (1994)	see above	see above	Greater appreciation of ethnic culture
Garrett, Griffiths, James & Scholfield (1994)	see above	see above	Significant increases in positive attitudes towards own ethnic group
Geer (1981)	n=48 Korean Americans, ages 10-14	attendence at Korean schools for 2 yrs vs. all English	attendees had more postive attitude toward ethnic group, closer identification with Koreans, higher Korean prof.

Study	Sample	Treatment	Results
Lambert & Cazabon (1994)	see above	see above	Majority made friends with students in other language group, believe they know how members of other group think and feel, like school with both languages.
Landry & Allard (1991)	n=725 grade 12 Fr. Canadians	French language schools, 1-12	More HL support, contact related to greater ethnic vitality.
Soh (1993)	n=161 Chinese Singaporean jr college students	Bilingual schools (Chinese-English) vs. English only	Bilingual had more positive attitudes toward own & other ethnic groups
Walker de Félix & Peña (1992)	see above	see above	more positive attitudes toward Mexicans, increased awareness of ethnic backround
Xidis (1993)	see above	see above	more positive attitude toward Greek culture, greater cultural understanding
Self-Evaluation			
Feuerverger (1994)	see above	see above	minimized culture shock greater confidence, pride in HL

Study	Sample	Treatment	Results
Fisher (1974)	n=28 grade 1 in bil. ed. 14 Chicano, 14 Anglo	bilingual ed. 7 months	Chicano girls: increase in self-image. Control girls did not feel like important members of the class, ill more often
Garrett, Griffiths, James & Scholfield (1994)	see above	see above	increase in positive self-ratings
Hornberger (1988)	Queckhua speaking children in Peru	Spanish only vs. bilingual education	Spanish only: more stress, under participation self-ratings misbehavior, reticence
Walker de Félix & Peña (1992)	see above	see above	greater sense of personal power

LANGUAGE ATTITUDE

Positive attitudes toward the target language have been found to be a significant predictor of success in language acquisition (see Gardner, 1985 for a review). In light of the importance of language attitudes, it is necessary to examine if and to what extent heritage language programs affect those attitudes. The studies discussed below suggest that heritage language contact may have dramatic impact on minority students' attitudes toward the language, and their appreciation of and confidence in using the language.

Several studies available on HL programs and language attitudes compare existing groups of ethnic minority students, some who have exposure to heritage language programs and others who do not.[2] One such study is by Xidis (1993) who compared the language attitudes of two groups of 7th and 8th grade Greek Americans. One group of students ($n = 75$) was enrolled in Greek language schools, including Greek day schools, ethnic schools, and bilingual education programs. A second group ($n = 66$) attended English-language public schools. To discover whether these groups were comparable, a re-analysis of Xidis' data was conducted. The results show that the two groups did not differ significantly in terms of SES (mostly upper middle class) or the place of birth of the subjects (all but one U.S. born), but did differ in terms of parents' place of birth. Significantly more students with parents born abroad in Greece or another country attended Greek schools. These differences must be kept in mind in evaluating Xidis' results.

Xidis found through attitude questionnaires, school records, and a Greek proficiency test that the students attending Greek schools had higher academic achievement and, not surprisingly, higher levels of Greek proficiency. Of particular relevance here is his finding that the Greek school students had significantly more positive attitudes toward the Greek language than their English-school counterparts on questions such as "Do you feel it is important for you to learn the Greek language?" and "How important is it for Greek Americans to learn the Greek language?". The subjects attending Greek schools, nearly all of whom (90%) had had Greek instruction for more than seven years, appeared to have retained positive attitudes toward the language and culture despite the strong forces of language shift (Fishman, 1991; Wong-Filmore, 1991), and have developed high levels of proficiency in the language at no expense to general academic performance. Whether those positive attitudes are a result of heritage language schooling itself or other factors cannot be determined due to the significant differences in the two groups compared. However, these results are suggestive when considered along side other similar findings, such as those in the studies discussed below.

Feuerverger (1989) also compared ethnic minority children in terms of the amount of exposure to the heritage language, although all of the students in her study had had some amount of instruction in the HL. Using a survey, she compared the attitudes of Italian Canadian eighth-graders in two Toronto schools, one with an integrated Italian HL program within the regular school day, and the other offering Italian classes on Saturday mornings. Significant differences were found between the schools with and without integrated programs in terms of how students rated the language's status and those students' own language ability. Especially worthy of note are the results of one particular class. Among the three groups that constituted the integrated program sample was a French immersion class that offered substantially more instruction in French, and the same amount of Italian instruction (with instruction in French (50%), English (40%), and Italian (10%), as compared to the other integrated classes with instruction in English (80%), French (10%), and Italian (10%)). These students had the most positive attitudes toward Italian and French and the greatest confidence in both their Italian and French literacy skills when compared to all of the other groups. In contrast, Feuerverger found strong feelings among the students in the afterschool program that Italian was not a legitimate school subject because it was not part of the "official" school curriculum. Interestingly, only one student out of the 67 potential subjects from the integrated HL program group chose not to participate in the study, while 23 out of 67 possible subjects from the non-integrated program group declined to participate. The high non-participation rate among the non-integrated group students may suggest that less exposure to the language and the lower degree of priority given to it in the school resulted in greater apathy toward the heritage language among those Italian Canadian students.

Positive attitudes toward studying academic subjects in the heritage language were found in a study by Muller, Penner, Bowers, Jones, and Mosychuk (1976) that compared the language attitudes and proficiency of 70 first-grade Ukrainian Canadian students enrolled in a bilingual education program (50% English and 50% Ukrainian instruction) and those attending English public schools. The students were given English and Ukrainian proficiency tests at the end of the first grade and some of the parents and students were interviewed. Unfortunately, the researchers did not provide sufficient information to determine whether significant differences existed between the two groups. In addition, only limited data were gathered from the students themselves regarding affect, perhaps due to their young age. Despite these limitations, Muller et al. found that a large majority (80%) of the students said that they liked doing work in Ukrainian and 70% wanted to enroll in the same program the following year. Proficiency tests of the two groups found that the bilingual education students had similar English language ability as their English school counterparts, with the bilingual education students performing significantly better than the English school group in a test of Ukrainian oral ability.

Looking at the attitudes of slightly older students in a two-way Spanish-English bilingual program, Lambert and Cazabon (1994) surveyed students in a Massachusetts school. The researchers found that these fourth, fifth, and sixth graders, like the children in Feuerverger's study, developed confidence in both their native and second languages, and had generally positive attitudes toward dual language learning. A large majority of the 57 students reported high levels of oral and literacy language ability, and all of the Spanish native speakers and all but 3 of the English native speakers wanted to continue learning Spanish. These children also developed favorable attitudes toward the other language group, as will be discussed in the next section.

Measuring the effects of a much more modest heritage language intervention, Garrett, Griffiths, James, and Scholfield (1994) tested whether a 12-week, one hour per week HL program would affect writing ability as well as students' attitudes toward language, school, and themselves. Students ages 10 and 11 dominant in either Welsh or Punjabi (the minority languages) in two cities in England were included in the sample. The groups performed pre-writing activities in their normally scheduled English writing lesson either in their heritage language ($n = 28$) or in English ($n = 28$). The children's attitudes and performance were measured with pre- and post-treatment attitude questionnaires and writing tasks. Although the results showed significant changes in other affective attitudes (see below), no differences in students' attitudes toward the HL, English, or bilingualism were found. The researchers suggest that the treatment may have been too short to produce effects and/or that the instrument was not sensitive enough to detect small changes. Similarly, no significant differences were found in the students' writing ability as a result of the intervention. Again, the researchers acknowledge the limitations of a short treatment period and point to bilingual education studies (e.g. Ramirez, 1992) showing that positive effects only become detectable after a longer period of exposure.

Another limited heritage language intervention program did produce improved language attitudes. Feuerverger (1994) described the effects of exposing minority and majority students to heritage language books in one Toronto school serving students from over a dozen language backgrounds. HL books were added to the school library and students were encouraged to read them in the library and to check them out to take home. Teachers were also allowed to borrow them for classroom use. Through in-depth interviews, participant observations (at school and in student homes), and periodic video-taping of five classrooms, Feuerverger noted marked positive changes in both the language minority and majority children's feelings toward the various HLs. Both groups developed an appreciation for the books and languages, and as further discussion of the study below shows, the language minority children gained other affective benefits in terms of ethnic group attitudes and self-esteem.

To summarize, HL programs appear to have positive impact on language attitudes in all but one of the studies, suggesting beneficial outcomes from exposure to and/or instruction in the language. The subjects reported greater appreciation of the heritage language, confidence in using it, enjoyment in doing school work in the language, and desire to continue learning it. The following section reviews the impact of HL programs on students' attitudes toward ethnic groups.

ETHNIC GROUP ATTITUDES

A number of studies have found that individuals who judge their ethnic group favorably and/or rate its members more positively than relevant comparison groups have more positive attitudes toward the heritage language and/or have higher proficiency in the language (Tse, forthcoming). In light of these findings and those of the previous section, it is important to examine whether and in what way HL exposure affects attitudes toward the ethnic group. The studies reviewed below suggest that this type of exposure affects both student views of their own ethnic group and their attitudes toward members of other language groups.

Several studies examine the relationship between heritage language program participation and subjects' views of their own ethnic group. Lambert, Giles, and Picard (1975) used matched guise techniques to examine the language and ethnic group attitudes of French American elementary school students in Maine, one group ($n = 32$) enrolled in a four-year bilingual education program and another group ($n = 36$) without any formal French instruction. The students listened to taped passages read in several varieties of English and French and were asked to rate the speakers on semantic differential adjective scales. The researchers found that the bilingual education group rated upper class French over any variety of English and were thus thought to aspire to the middle class French Canadian group. The no-French-instruction group rated English higher than any variety of French and they were therefore believed to aspire to the English-speaking model. As with several of the studies reviewed earlier, no attitudinal data were provided on these students prior to their enrollment in their respective schools, although the researchers note that "the program staff is convinced that they were essentially taken at random from a common pool to be placed in the Program or No Program group" (p. 142). If we assume this to be true, the findings suggest that exposure to an HL program promotes closer identification with one's own ethnic group, and minimizes the desire to join the (more powerful and higher status) majority language group.

Similar findings were discovered in a study by Landry and Allard (1991) who surveyed 725 grade 12 French native speakers in eight Canadian schools. All of the respondents had had French as the language of instruction since first grade. Landry and Allard found that the greater the educational support for the heritage language in a school, the more HL contact the students had in and out of school. In addition, the larger the heritage language community, the closer the subjects identified with the French Canadian ethnic group (as opposed to English-Canadians) and the higher their ratings of their ethnic group's "ethnolinguistic vitality." Ethnolinguistic vitality refers to an individual's evaluation of a group's status, demography, and institutional support (Giles, Bourhis, and Taylor, 1977). Not surprisingly, the researchers also found that the smaller the population of an ethnic community, the more important school support of the heritage language for positive HL and ethnic group attitudes was. Higher levels of educational support and greater amount of heritage language contact were also associated with heritage language and English language ability.

In Feuerverger's (1989) study mentioned above, the students with greater heritage language exposure also judged their own ethnic group as having higher levels of ethnolinguistic vitality than other ethnic groups on Likert questionnaires. The results showed that students with greater access to the heritage language had significantly more positive perceptions of the ethnic group's ethnolinguistic vitality and had significantly closer identification with the Italian ethnic group.

In Garrett, Griffiths, James, and Scholfield's (1994) 12-week study (see above) of students with and without heritage language instruction, the results revealed that those students with exposure to the language had significantly more favorable attitudes toward their own ethnic group associations at the end of the treatment period, in contrast to the English activity group whose views of their own ethnic identity remained the same or grew more distant. In Feuerverger's (1994) study where HL books were added to the school library, the students also appeared to develop greater appreciation for the ethnic culture and more positive attitudes toward the ethnic group.

Blake, Lambert, Sidoti, and Wolfe (1981) examined the ethnic group attitudes of English- and French Canadian students attending single-language schools and two-way immersion schools. The 360 children ages 6 and 11 were given attitude surveys. The results showed that the students attending immersion schools viewed French and English Canadians to be more similar to each other younger in life, and the bilingual students made more friends with children in other ethnic groups earlier in life than their monolingual counterparts. In addition, the older bilingual children had more suggestions and showed greater creativity in finding ways to alleviate tensions between the two ethnic groups.

In a study examining the effects of an heritage language program on adults, Walker de Félix and Peña (1992) gave pre- and post-treatment attitude surveys and Spanish proficiency tests to 16 Spanish-English bilingual teachers participating in a four-week study abroad program to Mexico. The teachers, all Mexican Americans, took part in language training and cultural sightseeing. The one-month experience appeared to have some dramatic effects on the teachers views of the ethnic group and culture, and on their views of themselves as Mexican Americans, as indicated on semantic differential questionnaires. The participants reported significantly more positive attitudes toward Mexicans and becoming more interested in and developing greater appreciation for their ethnic heritage. One of the students wrote in a journal entry:

"Se me enchinó el cuerpo al pisar esos lugares tan antiguos y saber que algo tengo en común con la gente que los fundó." (I got goose pimples all over when I walked around such ancient places knowing that I have something in common with the people that founded them.) (p. 747)

Another participant wrote:

"Hoy me puse a pensar que las influencias indígenas se notan en mi vida por parte de mis padres y abuelos." (Today I thought about how my parents and grandparents' Indian influences are noticeable in my life.) (p. 747)

This relatively brief program appeared to have resulted in greater appreciation of the participants' own cultural background and effected increased identification with the ethnic group.

Greater cultural understanding was also reported in Xidis' study (1993) of grade 7 and 8 Greek American students. Compared to other Greek American students of the same age attending no HL programs, these students showed more positive attitudes toward the Greek culture and reported greater appreciation of their cultural heritage, as measured on survey questionnaires.

In a number of the studies on affect, significantly different groups are compared, rendering the results somewhat difficult to interpret. Geer (1981) attempted to address this shortcoming by controlling for several factors, including SES (i.e. parents' educational background and occupations), immigration status, and perhaps most importantly, parents' willingness to enroll their children in HL schools. She was able to control for this last variable by including children from two different but somewhat comparable cities in New York—one city with heritage language programs and the other without. She only included those children in the no-HL program city whose parents indicated their desire to enroll their children in heritage language programs if they were available.

Her subjects consisted of 20 children who had attended heritage language school for at least two years and 28 non-HL school attendees, ranging from ages 10 to 14. Using an attitude questionnaire and tests of Korean language proficiency, Geer asked the children about their attitudes toward the Korean and Korean American ethnic groups, their ethnic identification, their attitudes toward the language, and assessed their Korean language proficiency.

Geer reported several interesting findings:

(1) The HL group had significantly more positive attitudes toward the ethnic group in general than did the non-HL group;

(2) The HL group reported significantly closer identification with Korean Americans than Americans; the non-HL group was, for the most part, ambivalent;

(3) The HL group felt that Korean Americans were more successful than other Americans; The non-HL group was again ambivalent;

(4) Combining the two groups, the older children (ages 12, 13, and 14) tended to be more ambivalent and negative toward the ethnic group and language than the younger children (ages 10 and 11);

(5) The HL group had significantly higher HL oral and written ability than the non-HL group.

Although this study did not control for all selection-related factors (e.g. language spoken at home), it attempted to control for a number of relevant factors and is among the most methodologically sound studies of its kind. For that reason, several tentative conclusions may be drawn from the results. For these students, heritage language school attendance appears to promote positive ethnic group and language attitudes, closer identification with the ethnic American group, and greater proficiency in the heritage language. The non-attendees indicated neutral opinions toward many of these same factors and reported a stronger identification with non-Korean Americans, which may reflect a general distancing and disassociation from the ethnic (Korean) and ethnic-American (Korean American) groups. The impact of HL programs reported in this study is particularly impressive when we consider the likely strong forces of language shift in these relatively small Korean communities in New York. In small ethnic communities, demographic concentration and institutional support are likely to be low, resulting in strong pressures to adopt majority culture and language (Fishman, Gertner, Lowry, and Milán, 1985; Fishman, 1991).

Lambert and Cazabon's (1994) study reported above found heritage language exposure to be positively related to both children's attitudes toward their own group as well as opinions of other groups with whom they have contact. Although no comparison group was used, a large majority of the elementary school subjects reported making friends with students from the other language group and indicated in a survey that they preferred having friends from both Spanish and English language backgrounds. Most of the students also liked being in a school with speakers of both languages, with less than 10% of the Spanish speakers preferring an all-English instruction school. When asked whether they knew how members of the other language group thought and felt, 75% of the native English speakers and over 80% of the native Spanish speakers answered that they did, suggesting that intercultural contact may promote mutual understanding. Similar results were obtained in a study by Soh (1993) who compared the ethnic group attitudes of 161 Chinese Singaporean junior college students, 84 of whom had attended Special Assistance Plan schools (SAP) and 77 of whom had attended English-language schools. The SAP schools were established to preserve the heritage language and to promote both English and Chinese as first languages. In a survey, the SAP participants indicated significantly more positive attitudes toward their own ethnic group and toward members of other language groups when compared to the non-SAP group.

The studies reviewed in this section suggest several effects of HL programs on ethnic group attitudes. The language minority subjects in
these programs appear to have more positive perceptions of the group
itself, greater appreciation of the ethnic culture, closer identification
with the ethnic group, and stronger belief that the ethnic group is desirable. HL program participants also appear to develop positive attitudes toward other groups. HL students have more friendships with
members of other language groups, perceive less social distance
between ethnic groups, and feel they understand other group members
better. Knowing some of the effects of heritage language programs on
language and ethnic group attitudes, we now turn to the question of
how exposure to the HL affects students' perceptions of themselves.

SELF-EVALUATION

Like language and ethnic group attitudes, one's attitudes and evaluations toward oneself have been found to be related to second language
achievement (e.g. Oller, Hudson, and Liu, 1977). Several of the studies
looking at self-evaluation compare the attitudes and behaviors of students in HL programs with those without heritage language exposure.
One such study is Hornberger's (1988) investigation in which attitudes
and behaviors of Quechua elementary school children in a Spanish-
only school were compared with children enrolled in a maintenance
bilingual education (Quechua-Spanish) school in Peru. Hornberger
made participant observations and tape recordings of class sessions
and found that the minority children in the Spanish-only school suf-
fered far more stress than those in the bilingual education program.
She observed that the Spanish-only school children were substantially
more reticent than the children in the other school and they participated less in class. The children in Spanish-only school also misbehaved
more, with some of the children disrupting classroom activities. As a
result, these children were put down verbally more often by the teacher
and punished far more than the children in the bilingual education program. Hornberger speculated that these behaviors were ways in which
children dealt with the stress of being in a school that did not provide
them with language support, validation of the home culture, and
teacher empathy.

Fisher (1974) also found these types of behavior in children without
bilingual education in his study of Latino and Anglo students. Fisher
collected pre- and post-treatment self-concept ratings of students in a
seven-month bilingual education project ($n = 28$) and those receiving
no instruction in the heritage language ($n = 39$). The results showed
that the Latina girls in the experimental group showed significant
improvements in their self-concept ratings, although no differences

were found for the boys. The Latino children in the control group reported not feeling like important members of the class, were out of school ill more often, and were involved in more fights.

Feuerverger's (1994) study shows that a relatively modest intervention can make a difference in students' self-esteem. As previously noted, HL books were added to the school library and use of those books was encouraged by the librarian and teachers. Feuerverger noted three affective outcomes of the project. First, the books were a source of comfort for some recently arrived students still growing accustomed to the majority school setting. Feuerverger observed that "it is as if initially, the books are like a security blanket. I myself saw how lovingly some of the children would hold these books" (p. 135). The librarian made similar observations and recounted an incident in which a newly arrived Iranian student—upon finding books in the library in Farsi— overcame some of his language apprehensions, joined in with the library activities along with the other students, and befriended an Iranian American student.

A second outcome of the project relates to the ethnic minority students who were given opportunities to share HL books with their fellow students, including reading aloud to them. Some of those students interviewed by Feuerverger appeared to have developed tremendous pride in their heritage language and in their own language ability as well as in their cultural heritage. Feuerverger described an interview with Alex, an 8-year-old from Bulgaria:

> He said that he read a story in Bulgarian to his grade three class and they all enjoyed it: "They asked me all kinds of questions. One boy said he wished he could have the book; another asked whether he could have it. Everyone laughed because it was a funny story. Some of them tried to say the words in Bulgarian but they couldn't." His confidence was glowing as he translated the story for me into English. (p. 137)

The books also served as a bridge between home and school, and between limited-English-proficient parents and their children. One parent commented: "The children bring books in Farsi home to read. Such a good idea. We can explain what our world was like to them while we read. It brings us close together" (p. 140). This program not only promoted HL development, but brought about school validation of the students' linguistic and cultural backgrounds. Moreover, the incorporation of the HL books created an atmosphere of multiculturalism and multilingualism that promoted positive language attitudes and high levels of confidence and self-esteem in the language minority students.

In another limited intervention study, Garrett, Griffiths, James, and Scholfield (1994) (described above) tested the effectiveness of a 12-week, one hour per week intervention on Welsh and Punjabi children's self-evaluation. The researchers found that there were significant increases in the students' ratings of themselves, while the attitudes of the students receiving no heritage language instruction remained the same or grew more negative. Walker de Félix and Peña's (1992) one-month intervention (also described above) revealed that the bilingual teachers who were exposed to the heritage language and culture in a travel abroad program also had increases in self-evaluation, including feelings of increased personal power. While these findings are admittedly limited, taken together with the other results showing positive outcomes in terms of improved ethnic identity and language attitudes, they suggest that even limited HL interventions—both in time and scope—can effect some significant and positive attitudinal changes.

Conclusions and Suggestions for Further Research

The studies reviewed in this paper suggest that given contact with the heritage language in an environment that is supportive of its development, positive attitudinal changes can be effected. These results indicate that ethnic minority individuals may benefit from heritage language development. The most positive attitudes seem to be in those students who are in programs sanctioned by their day school and are integrated into the regular school curriculum. It is likely that students who perceive their school as recognizing the importance and value of having first language ability also develop such opinions. For this reason, community HL programs may not be able to promote the same high levels of interest and positive attitudes that day school programs would, although more investigation is needed.

A number of gaps remain in the literature and further research is needed in several areas to determine the best ways to go about providing heritage language exposure. First, the majority of these studies focus on elementary school students, with only a few looking at junior high, high school, and college-aged students. It is unknown whether interventions work differently with students at different ages. Second, more research is needed on the effectiveness of various methods of providing heritage language exposure. Although many types of HL programs have been included in this review, the lack of detailed program description makes it difficult to determine which factors actually effected the positive changes. Attention to program features in future studies may shed light on this question. Third, to determine the long term effects of an intervention, longitudinal attitude data are necessary to ensure that the programs have lasting effects. Finally, recent studies suggest that attitudes toward the HL may be developmental and include periods of negative heritage language attitudes in childhood and adolescence (Tse, this volume). Integrated HL programs may be able to minimize the effects of those stages and promote more positive attitudes. This possibility, however, has not been explored.

Despite the positive impact of heritage language programs, Fishman (1991) has noted that "without considerable and repeated societal reinforcement," long term HL development is unlikely (p. 371). Only when bilingualism and HL proficiency are valued by majority culture and seen as an asset to both majority and minority groups will heritage language development be widespread, and active promotion cease to be necessary. Until then, however, schools can play an important role in giving students the support they need to develop positive attitudes that will increase their chances of HL acquisition and allow them to experience the benefits of bilingualism.

Notes

1. A version of this chapter also appears in the Canadian Modern Language Review. (1997) **53:** 705-728

2. It is possible that students who voluntarily attend heritage language programs may be positively biased in affective outcomes. However, there is some evidence suggesting that participation in HL programs is often not voluntary, but rather compelled by parents (Brook, 1988).

References

Blake, L., Lambert, W.E., Sidoti, N., and Wolfe, D. (1981) "Students' views of intergroup tensions in Quebec: The effects of language immersion experience." *Canadian Journal of Behavioral Science* **13(2):** 144–160.

Brook, K.L. (1988) "Language Maintenance in the Japanese American Community" (M.A. Thesis, California State University, Long Beach, 1988). *Dissertation Abstracts International*.

Crawford, J. (1991) *Bilingual Education: History, Politics, Theory, and Practices* (2nd ed.). Los Angeles: Bilingual Educational Services.

Feuerverger, G. (1989) "Ethnolinguistic vitality of Italo-Canadian students in integrated and non-integrated heritage language programs in Toronto." *The Canadian Modern Language Review* **46(1):** 50–72.

Feuerverger, G. (1994) "A multicultural literacy intervention for minority language students." *Language and Education* **8(3):** 123–146.

Fisher, R.I. (1974) "A study of non-intellectual attributes of children in first grade bilingual-bicultural program." *The Journal of Educational Research* **67(7):** 323–328.

Fishman, J., Gertner, M.H., Lowry, E.G., and Milán, W.G. (1985) *Ethnicity in Action: The Community Resources of Ethnic Languages in the United States.* Binghamton, NY: Bilingual Press.

Fishman, J. (1991) *Reversing Language Shift.* Clevedon: Multilingual Matters.

Gardner, R.C. (1985) *Social Psychology and Second Language Learning.* London: Edward Arnold Publications.

Gardner, R.C., and Lambert, W.E. (1972) *Attitudes and Motivation in Second-Language Learning.* Rowley, MA: Newbury House.

Garrett, P., Griffiths, Y., James, C., and Scholfield, P. (1994) "Use of the mother-tongue in second language classrooms: An experimental investigation of effects on the attitudes and writing performance of bilingual UK schoolchildren." *Journal of Multilingual and Multicultural Development* **15(5):** 371–383.

Geer, C.H.S. (1981) "Korean Americans and Ethnic Heritage Education: A Case Study in Western New York" (Doctoral dissertation, State University of New York at Buffalo, 1981. *Dissertation Abstracts International*, 42, 3896.

Giles, H. and Byrne, J.L. (1982) "An intergroup approach to second language acquisition." *Journal of Multilingual and Multicultural Development* **3:** 17–40.

Giles, H., Taylor, D., and Bourhis, R. (1977) "Dimensions of Welsh Identity." *European Journal of Social Psychology* **7:** 165-174

Harris, B. (1980) "How a three-year-old translates." In E.A. Afendras (Ed.), *Patterns of Bilingualism* (pp. 371–393). Singapore: Singapore University Press.

Hornberger, N.H. (1988) "Misbehaviour, punishment and put-down: Stress for Quechua children in school." *Language and Education* **2(4)**: 239–253.

Krashen, S. (1981) *Second Language Acquisition and Second Language Learning.* New York: Prentice Hall.

Krashen, S. (1985) *The Input Hypothesis: Issues and Implications.* Beverly Hills: Laredo.

Lambert, W.E., and Cazabon, M. (1994) *Students' views of the Amigos Program Report No. 11.* Santa Cruz, CA: National Center for Research on Cultural Diversity and Second Language Learning.

Lambert, W.E., Giles, H., and Picard, O. (1975) "Language attitudes in a French-American community." *Linguistics* **158**: 127–152.

Landry, R. (1974) "A comparison of second language learners and monolinguals on divergent thinking tasks at the elementary school level." *Modern Language Journal* **58**: 10–15.

Landry, R. and Allard, R. (1991) "Can schools promote additive bilingualism in minority group children?" In L. Malavé, and G. Duquette (Eds.), *Language, Culture, and Cognition: A Collection of Studies in First and Second Language Acquisition* (pp. 198–231). Clevedon: Multilingual Matters.

Muller, L.J., Penner, W.J., Blowers, T.A., Jones, J.P., and Mosychuk, H. (1976) "Evaluation of a bilingual (English-Ukrainian) program." *Canadian Modern Language Review* **33(4)**: 476–485.

Oller, J.W. Jr., Hudson, A.J., and Liu, P.F. (1977) "Attitudes and attained proficiency in ESL: A sociolinguistic study of native speakers of Chinese in the United States." *Language Learning* **27(1)**: 1–27.

Ramirez, J.D. (1992) "Executive summary." *Bilingual Research Journal* **16(1-2)**: 1–62.

Soh, K.C. (1992) "Language motivation and ethnic attitude of high-ability students who attended ethnically homogeneous secondary schools." *Language and Education* **7(4)**: 271–281.

Taylor, D.M., Bassili, J.N., and Aboud, F.E. (1973) "Dimensions of ethnic identity: An examination from Quebec." *Journal of Social Psychology* **89**: 185–192.

Tse, L. "An examination of the relationship between ethnic identification and attitudes toward the ethnic language: Toward a developmental model." Forthcoming.

Walker de Félix, J., and Peña, S.C. (1992) "Return home: The effects of study in Mexico on bilingual teachers." *Hispania* **75(3):** 743–750.

Wong-Filmore, L. (1991) "When learning a second language means losing the first." *Early Childhood Research Quarterly* **6:** 323–346.

Xidis, A.S. (1993) "The Impact of Greek Bilingual Programs on the Academic Performance, Language Preservation, and Ethnicity of Greek-American Students: A Case Study in Chicago" (Doctoral dissertation, Florida State University, 1993) *Dissertation Abstracts International*, 54, 416.

6. The Use of Self-Selected and Free Voluntary Reading in Heritage Language Programs: A Review of Research

Jeff McQuillan

The number of secondary schools and universities offering courses designed especially for heritage language (HL) speakers has increased dramatically in recent years (Collisten, 1994). Despite the appearance of a number of theoretical frameworks on how to approach HL instruction (Valdes, 1995; Merino, Trueba, and Sanmaniego, 1993) and the publication of several textbooks and proposed curricula ranging from traditional grammar instruction (Gonzales and Gonzales, 1991; Blanco, 1994; Sole, 1994) to communicative approaches (Roca, 1994), there has been little formal evaluation of the effectiveness of any of these methods.

One exception is a small body of research on the promotion of self-selected, pleasure reading—what Krashen (1993) calls "free voluntary reading" (FVR)—in HL classes. This chapter reviews the literature on the use of FVR and self-selected reading with HL students, and discuss at what age and under what conditions HL courses may be most effective.

Access, Free Voluntary Reading, and Heritage Language Acquisition

Studies of language minority students in the United States have found that HL speakers often have extremely limited access to HL reading materials at home, in school, and in the community (Constantino, 1994; McQuillan, in press; Pucci, 1994). Research has shown that more access to books leads to more reading, and more reading results in higher levels of grammatical accuracy, a larger vocabulary, and greater reading comprehension (Krashen, 1993). One of the principle challenges in maintaining and developing HL literacy, then, is increasing access to interesting, comprehensible HL texts in a low-risk environment.

Teachers have different options in providing students access to comprehensible reading materials. Table 1 lists three possibilities, labeled according to current use of these terms.[1]

Table 1
Options in Providing Comprehensible Reading

Type	Self-Selected?	Accountability?
Sustained Silent Reading	yes	no
"Literature"	no	yes
"Self-Selected Reading"	yes	yes

All three methods can be successful if they provide interesting, comprehensible texts to students. Sustained silent reading (SSR), where students select their own reading materials and are not held accountable for what they read, has been found to be consistently effective (Krashen, 1993). "Literature," traditionally assigned reading that students are graded on, can work if texts are sufficiently interesting to the students (McQuillan and Conde, 1996). The third option, "Self-Selected Reading," where students choose the books but are evaluated in some way on their reading (e.g. keeping a reading log, writing a report), can also be effective if accountability is kept to a minimum.

Research on programs which increase access to texts and promote self-selected and free reading among HL students confirms that this approach can indeed be very successful. Table 2 summarizes the results of seven studies of reading programs which included these elements for HL (Spanish/English) bilinguals. (Note that while "heritage language" students are usually those who have already acquired English, I have also included one study, Schon, Hopkins and Davis (1982), which used students in an elementary bilingual program.)

Elementary and Secondary School Studies

In this first study in table 2, Schon, Hopkins and Davis (1982), free reading was provided to elementary Spanish/English bilingual students via a sustained silent reading program. The six experimental group teachers gave their second, third, and fourth grade HL students at least sixty minutes per week to read on their own in Spanish, or an average of about ten minutes per day, for eight months. The classes were provided with an extensive collection of Spanish language books selected for their high interest and easy texts. The control group participated in

Table 2

Studies Comparing HL Instruction Using Self-Selected/Sustained Silent Reading
and Traditional Approaches for Spanish/English Bilinguals

Study	Subjects	Measure	Results
Schon, Hopkins & Davis (1982)	2nd-4th graders n = 93	RC Vocab. Attitudes toward reading	Grade 2: SSR superior in vocab. equivalent in RC Grades 3.4: SSR superior on vocab. and RC Combined grades: SSR superior on attitudes toward reading
Schon, Hopkins & Vojir (1985)	7th-8th graders n = 400	RC Vocab. Attitudes	Grade 8: SSR superior in vocab.; equivalent on all other measures
Schon, Hopkins & Vojir (1984) (Tempe)	9th-12th graders n = 68	RC Attitudes	Equivalent gains for both SSR and traditional groups
Schon, Hopkins & Vojir (1984) (Chandler)	10th-12th graders n = 30	RC Attitude	Equivalent gains for both SSR and traditional groups
Rodrigo (1995)	University students n = 6	Vocab. Attitudes	Gains in vocab. and more positive attitudes; no controls
McQuillan (1996)	University students n = 39	Vocab. Attitudes	Equivalent on HL attitudes; significant gains in vocab. (no control group on vocab.)
McQuillan (1996)	University students n = 28	Amount of HL reading	SSR group reading more 7 months after treatment than comparison group

RC = reading comprehension

the regular language arts curriculum of the school during these same sixty minutes. Schon et al. report that all of the children in the study were primarily from low socio-economic areas of Tempe, Arizona. No information was provided as to the percentage of students who were Spanish dominant versus those who were English dominant.

The researchers found that five of the six experimental group teachers were very enthusiastic about the program, and that their students liked reading the books. One teacher commented that the students enjoyed "sharing stories with each other and reading aloud to the class" (p. 14). Standardized reading comprehension and vocabulary measures were administered before and after the treatment to both groups. The SSR group outscored the control classes in grade two on vocabulary (effect size = .63), and made equivalent gains in reading comprehension. For the third and fourth grade groups, the SSR students made significantly greater gains on both measures, with moderate to large effect sizes (.69 for reading comprehension, 1.1 for vocabulary). The analysis of the reading attitudes survey combined all three grades, and again the SSR group made significantly greater gains over the control group, with a modest effect size (.39).

In Schon, Hopkins and Vojir (1985), sixteen seventh- and eighth-grade remedial reading classes which contained both Mexican American students as well as recent immigrants were provided with access to popular Spanish reading materials and given 45 minutes of SSR each week in place of their regular English language arts time for eight and a half months. The control group students were the previous year's cohort of seventh- and eighth-graders, who received no SSR and did not have access to the Spanish materials. As in their other studies, Schon et al. asked the teachers to encourage bilingual students in the SSR groups to read in Spanish. The vast majority of the Spanish bilinguals came from low income areas in the city (Tempe, Arizona).

The researchers administered tests of Spanish reading comprehension, Spanish reading speed, Spanish vocabulary, and attitudes toward reading. In addition, the data were analyzed to investigate whether teacher assignment affected the outcomes, and whether those enrolled in a "Spanish for Native Speaker" (SNS) class responded more favorably to the treatment than those who were not.

Schon et al. report that the results of the intervention were mixed. The seventh-grade SSR groups did marginally better than the control groups on Spanish reading comprehension and vocabulary measures, but the differences were not statistically significant, and there were no differences on the reading attitudes subtests. For the eighth-grade groups, the SSR students did significantly better on the vocabulary and the reading speed test (effect sizes of .43 and .61 respectively), but not on reading comprehension or attitudes.

There were some reported problems with treatment fidelity in this study. Only five of the eleven teachers were found to be conscientious in carrying out the SSR program. A separate analysis of those teachers who were faithful to the program revealed that their students did significantly better than the other experimental group bilinguals on both Spanish vocabulary and reading speed by a substantial margin (effect sizes of .88 and 1.37, respectively). There was no reported interaction between those who were enrolled in the SNS course and the treatment.

Clearly the program was effective for some students, particularly when the teachers made a serious effort to implement the treatment. Unfortunately, Schon et al. do not report on the breakdown of immigrant-Mexican versus Mexican American students in their sample, which may have affected its results (see below). The failure to find any interaction among the treatment and SNS course enrollment is also an ambiguous finding, since we do not know if the SNS students were more likely to be recently arrived immigrants.

Schon, Hopkins and Vojir (1984) report on two studies of SSR used in high school (grades nine to twelve) remedial reading courses. In the first study (Tempe), teachers in the experimental groups were given Spanish books for their bilingual students to use during the approximately 12 minutes a day of their SSR time over a period of four months. With the help of a bilingual resource aide, the instructors were asked to encourage their interested students to read in Spanish during SSR. The control group students received no Spanish language texts. Eighty percent of both the experimental and control group students came from a low-income area of the city, but the school itself served students from a predominantly Anglo, high-income area. Pre- and post-treatment measures were administered for Spanish reading comprehension and attitudes toward reading. Schon et al. found no significant differences between the two groups on either measure.

There are plausible reasons why the SSR treatment failed to produce better gains in the study. First, Krashen (1993) has noted that SSR programs provide consistently superior results to traditional instruction when given at least seven months (almost a full school year) to operate. The Tempe study last only four months. Second, experimental group students could choose either English or Spanish for their SSR reading.

If their dominant language for reading was English, then many may have simply chosen not to read in Spanish at all. Third, it is clear from the comments of the experimental group teachers that the HL students found the Spanish books and materials provided them either too difficult or uninteresting. Several students told their teacher that "I can't read Spanish. How do you expect me to read these materials?" (p. 38). Finally, many of the high school bilinguals may not have been motivated to read in the HL for reasons related to ethnic identity conflicts (see below).

In Schon's second high school study (Chandler, Arizona), teachers used a similar SSR approach. Again, a majority of the Spanish bilinguals are reported to have been from a low socio-economic part of the school district, but the school consisted primarily of middle-income Anglo students. The SSR students were provided with materials similar to those of the Tempe study discussed above, but here the SSR treatment lasted seven months instead of four. Schon and her colleagues reported no significant differences between the two groups on either the reading comprehension or the reading attitudes survey.

There are again some possible reasons why the SSR approach failed to produce positive results. The researchers point out that some of the teachers involved in the SSR treatment were not actually implementing it in their classrooms, thus making the comparisons between methods suspect. Further, the researchers reported that a number of students in the control group found out about the Spanish materials given to the experimental group and (voluntarily) began reading the experimental group's books and newspapers. The results of this study need, then, to be treated with caution.

What is interesting about both the Tempe and the Chandler studies, however, are the dramatic differences in how the U.S.-born Mexican American students and the more recently arrived, Mexican-born immigrants reacted to the Spanish reading materials made available to them. Schon and her colleagues reported that:

> [The] U.S.-born Hispanic students were not interested in reading in Spanish and rarely if ever used the specially provided reading materials in Spanish ... The responses of the Hispanics born in Mexico was quite different, however. They often read the Spanish materials provided and eagerly awaited the weekly *El Sol* newspaper.

> The responses of the U.S.-born Hispanics tended to be apathetic and passively hostile. In fact, many of the *CTBS Espanol* post-test scores in [the Chandler study] are obviously invalid due to lack of cooperation. (For example, scores went from about 50% on the pre-test to near 0% on the post-test). (Schon et al., 1984, pp. 36–37)

One teacher stated that "Mexican-American students are *embarrassed* about these books in Spanish. They don't want to look at them—they stay far away from them," while the "minority who come from Mexico are interested in them" (p. 38, emphasis added). Other teachers reported similar reactions among the experimental group students.

This lack of interest in HL materials is consistent with Tse's (this volume) four stage developmental model of ethnic identity formation. Tse found evidence among visible ethnic minorities that those who desire to join the majority group often go through predictable stages in coping with their ethnic identity, and that this process has important implications for their attitudes toward the HL. In stage 2 of Tse' s model, Ethnic Ambivalence/Evasion, ethnic minorities strive to identify themselves with the majority culture and as a consequence become ambivalent or even hostile toward associations with their HL. Tse notes that Stage 2 often takes place sometime during childhood and adolescence, which appears to be the case for the Mexican American students in Schon et al.'s studies.

Tse's model also predicts that this type of distancing from the HL will not affect those who still have strong ties to the heritage culture or who, for reasons of language or other social barriers, do not see integration into the majority group as possible. This again is precisely what Schon et al. report: the recently arrived Mexican-born immigrants, who are less likely to be able to integrate in the majority group of the school due to linguistic barriers, are not averse to reading materials in their HL.[2] This confirmation of Tse's predictions concerning ethnic minority students' reactions to efforts to promote the HL has potentially important implications for the implementation of HL programs, as I will discuss below.

University Level Studies

There have been three studies conducted using self-selected and free reading programs with university HL students. Rodrigo (1995; reported in McQuillan and Rodrigo, in press), used a literature-based program in a 15 week, intermediate (fourth semester) Spanish course in a large, private university in the Los Angeles area. The course consisted mostly of English-only students, but included six native Spanish bilinguals, most of whom were English dominant. Only the results from the HL students will be discussed here. The class met twice a week for 80 minutes, during which time students could read self-selected texts quietly and discuss their readings with the instructor. There were two elements of the program:

(1) *Popular Literature:* This involved the use of assigned, easy to read popular literature books which are interesting and comprehensible to students (Dupuy, Tse and Cook, 1996). Students read six "graded" books written especially for non-native speakers and two abridged books for the course. The graded readers were all of a single genre— detective stories—in accordance with the recommendations of Krashen (1981) regarding "narrow reading," where students take advantage of cumulative background knowledge derived from reading several texts on a similar topic. The readings were discussed in class, and students did a short book report on each.

(2) *Self-Selected Reading:* Students read three books of their own choosing, having only to keep a log of the books they read. Students also did brief oral reports in class in the form of "reviews" to let others in the class know what they were reading. Texts included graded readers, children's books, adolescent fiction, comic books, newspapers, magazines, and a few literary works.

To evaluate the success of the program, Rodrigo created a vocabulary checklist similar to the type used by West and Stanovich (1991) to measure the amount of incidental vocabulary acquisition (Nagy, Herman and Anderson, 1985). The vocabulary list was created from several graded readers in Spanish, some of which were read by Rodrigo's students as part of their self-selected reading. The six bilingual students made an average gain of 6% on the test in the 15 week period, an impressive gain considering that no formal evaluation on the self-selected reading or vocabulary instruction was used during the course. The results are consistent with other data which suggest that vocabulary acquisition is largely incidental and is most efficiently achieved through reading, particularly pleasure reading, rather than through direct instruction (Krashen, 1993).

Rodrigo also administered an open-ended affective survey. Five of the six HL students said they enjoyed reading in Spanish more after taking the course, and all six felt that their competence in Spanish reading had improved over the 15 week semester. Some comments from open-ended questions on the survey included:

—I liked the fact that there was no testing ... I actually felt the results of my improved reading comprehension as [the program] was going on.

—The material was interesting in that it helped me gain a better handle on Spanish.

—By reading subjects that interested me, I grew to understand more about Latin American views and learn Spanish writing techniques I was not familiar with (Rodrigo, 1995).

I conducted two studies in Spanish for Native Speakers (SNS) courses using similar literature-based approaches (McQuillan, 1996). In the first study, the experimental class consisted of twenty mostly English-dominant bilingual students enrolled in a lower-division SNS course at a medium-sized public university in the Los Angeles area. The class met twice a week for three-hour sessions during the ten-week quarter. Students were placed in the course based on a mandatory placement exam administered by the university's foreign language department. The curriculum had two elements:

(1) *Survey of Popular Literature:* This was a type of extensive reading where students were given twenty readings representing a variety of genres of popular and classical Spanish literature in order to familiarize them with what was available for them to read for pleasure (Dupuy, Tse and Cook, 1996). The readings were discussed in class each week.

(2) *Literature Circles:* Students formed self-selected discussion groups at the beginning of the quarter and spent 20 minutes during each class period talking about a novel the group selected to read (MacGillivray, Tse and McQuillan, 1995; McQuillan and Tse, 1997).

The control group consisted of 19 students enrolled in another SNS class at the same university. Students received more traditional grammar work, but also read selections of literature during the course, minimizing somewhat the contrast with the experimental group.

As in Rodrigo (1995), incidental vocabulary growth was measured by a vocabulary checklist developed by Rodrigo (1994). The results indicated that the experimental group made significant gains in word knowledge during the quarter, averaging 8%. As in the case of Rodrigo's study above, this represents a substantial growth in vocabulary when we consider the short exposure to reading and the lack of any direct vocabulary instruction. The control group did not take the vocabulary test, however, so the gains cannot be compared to the more traditional approach.

Both groups were administered a survey on attitudes toward HL reading at the end of the course. The responses of the experimental group were slightly more positive with respect to the attitudes toward reading in the heritage language than the control group, although the differences were not statistically significant. It is important to remember that the control group in this study also did some reading, which may account for their increased confidence toward reading in the HL. In any case, the experimental treatment produced comparable results with respect to attitudes toward the HL as the grammar-based method.

In the second study, a slightly different approach was used with a similar class of university-level, largely English-dominant SNS students (*n* = 10). The course met for 10 weeks, six hours per week, and had three components:

(1) *Popular Literature Survey:* The same method as described in Study 1 above was used.

(2) *Outside Self-Selected Reading:* Students kept a log of their outside reading from newspapers, magazines, and books. Students selected their own reading, and were encouraged to read the equivalent of about 10 newspaper articles a week. During class, students were asked to comment on what they were reading and recommend readings to their classmates.

(3) *Individual Inquiry Learning Project:* Students selected one topic related to Latino/Chicano culture that interested them and then read materials in Spanish related to that topic. The purpose of the Inquiry Project was to encourage students to take advantage of "narrow reading" (Krashen, 1981). A short, written report on the topic was turned in at the end of the quarter.

The course also included short lectures on Mexican and Mexican American history to provide further background knowledge for some students' self-selected reading. Some very limited grammar instruction was also included, comprising less than 10% of class time.

None of the students reported regular pleasure reading in their heritage language before the course began. In order to measure the long-term effects of the experimental treatment, an anonymous survey was sent to the students seven months after the end of the quarter to see if they were still reading for pleasure. In order to provide for a comparison with similar students, a group of eighteen SNS students who had not participated in the literature-based treatment were also surveyed. As shown in Table 3, significantly more students in the experimental group reported that they were reading in Spanish after the end of the course than the comparison group of university Spanish bilinguals (Fisher Exact Test, Two Tail, $p < .05$).

Table 3
Do You Read for Pleasure in Spanish?

Group	yes	no
Experimental	90% (9)	10% (1)
Control	44% (8)	56% (10)

(from McQuillan, 1996, Table 4)

In addition, sixty percent of the experimental group reported that they were reading more now than before they took the experimental course.

The number of subjects in this study was small, and the results can only be suggestive. However, they are consistent with previous research showing that even a short exposure to self-selected and free reading approaches can have long-term effects on reading habits (Greaney and Clarke, 1973).

Implications: Access and Timing in HL Programs

Unlike other recommendations for HL programs, particularly those which argue for a more grammatically-based syllabus (e.g. Sole, 1994), the use of self-selected and free voluntary reading has empirical support as to its effectiveness with HL students. These results are consistent with a large body of research on the effects of free voluntary reading on literacy development in first and second language classrooms (Krashen, 1993).

The research reviewed here also gives us some preliminary evidence on when HL programs might be most effective. Tse's four stage model of ethnic identity development predicts that HL programs will only be effective if ethnic minority students are willing to associate themselves with their heritage culture, or at least not be ambivalent or hostile to it. This typically occurs when (a) they are largely unaware of ethnic differences, usually in early childhood (Tse's Stage 1); or (b) when they are in "ethnic emergence" and "incorporation," during which time they often attempt to learn more about their ethnic culture, usually in late adolescence or adulthood (Stages 3 and 4). Students in Stage 2 of Tse's model, ethnic ambivalence/evasion, will not respond favorably to attempts to promote the HL.

This is essentially the pattern we see in studies reviewed here on HL students: HL programs in the early elementary grades and university level were successful, while programs aimed at junior and senior high school students produced few positive results.[3] Of course, there were problems with the high school studies discussed here (treatment fidelity, program duration, text difficulty and interest), so these conclusions are necessarily tentative. If true, however, they would indicate that HL programs will be most effective if they are aimed at ethnic minority students in late adolescence or early adulthood, and promote group membership with the heritage culture (Tse, this volume).[4]

A practical problem in implementing free reading programs for HL students is providing students with materials to read that are both interesting and comprehensible. Dupuy and McQuillan (1997a, 1997b) have proposed that intermediate and advanced HL students can make their own reading material—"handcrafted books"—which can be read by students in lower or similar level classes. These student-generated books have the advantage of giving adult acquirers sophisticated content at a low linguistic level. The long-term solution, however, is that schools and universities provide a rich source of HL reading materials in the library, where they are easily accessible.

Notes

1. I thank Stephen Krashen for this classification of reading options.

2. Becker (1990) reports on a similar phenomenon among immigrant high school students from Portugal living in urban New England. The immigrant teens who had resided longer in the United States (six to sixteen years) distanced themselves from the more recent arrivals (less than two years of residence) to the point where earlier arrivals would only speak English, identify themselves as Anglos, and refuse to acknowledge that they could speak or understand any Portuguese. (All of the students spoke Portuguese at home, however, and still had high levels of proficiency.)

3. We do not know, however, the composition of the early elementary classes (Schon, Hopkins and Davis, 1982) in terms of language dominance or length of residence. It is conceivable that the majority of students who participated in the program were recently arrived, Spanish dominant immigrants who were therefore "outside" the Tse model, since they may not have (yet) aspired to become members of the majority group.

4. We may speculate that the Spanish language ability of the teachers had some impact on promoting group membership and hence success of the HL programs in these studies. In the clearly successful early elementary and university level studies (Schon, Hopkins and Davis, 1982; Rodrigo, 1995; McQuillan, 1996), 100% (7/7) of the SSR group teachers were bilingual (five Latinos and two Anglos). In the studies where the HL program produced mixed or poor results (Schon, Hopkins and Vojir, 1984), only 18% (3/11) of the SSR teachers spoke Spanish (all Latinos), the rest being monolingual Anglos.

References

Becker, A. (1980) "The role of the school in the maintenance and change of ethnic group affiliation." *Human Organization* **49:** 48–55.

Blanco, G. (1994) "El hispanohablante y la grammatica." *Bilingual Research Journal* **18:** 23–46.

Colliston, M. (1994) "Spanish for native speakers." *The Chronicle of Higher Education* **40 (22):** A15–A16.

Constantino, R. (1994) " 'It's like a lot of things in America': Linguistic minority parents' use of the public library." *School Library Media Quarterly* **23:** 87–89.

Dupuy, B., Tse, L. and Cook, T. (1996) "Bringing books into the classroom: First steps in turning college-level ESL students into readers." *TESOL Journal* **5:** 10–15.

Dupuy, B. and McQuillan, J. "Check this out!: Handcrafted books." *Canadian Modern Language Review.* (1997a) **53:** 743-747.

Dupuy, B. and McQuillan, J. (1997b) "Handcrafted books: Two for the price of one." In G. Jacobs, C. Davis, and W. Renandya (Eds.) *Successful Strategies for Extensive Reading.* Singapore: SEAMEO Regional Language Centre. pp. 171-180.

Gonzales, A. and Gonzales, M. (1991) *Espanol para El Hispanohablante en Los Estados Unidos.* New York: University Press of America.

Greaney, V. and Clarke, M. (1973) "A longitudinal study of the effects of two reading methods on leisure-time reading habits." In D. Moyle (Ed.), *Reading: What of the Future?* London: United Kingdom Reading Association. pp. 107–114.

Krashen, S. (1981) "The case for narrow reading." *TESOL Newsletter* **15**: 23.

Krashen, S. (1993) *The Power of Reading.* Englewood, CO: Libraries Unlimited.

MacGillivray, L., Tse, L., and McQuillan, J. (1995) "Second language and literacy teachers considering literature circles: A play." *Journal of Adolescent and Adult Literacy* **39**: 36–44.

McQuillan, J. (1996) "How should heritage languages be taught? The effects of a free voluntary reading program." *Foreign Language Annals* **29**: 56–72.

McQuillan, J. (In press) "Language minority students and public library use in the United States." *Public Library Quarterly.*

McQuillan, J. and Conde, G. (1996) "The conditions of flow in reading: Two studies of optimal experience." *Reading Psychology: An International Quarterly* **17**: 109–135.

McQuillan, J. and Rodrigo, V. "Setting up literature-based programs for first language development: Access to books for native Spanish bilinguals." In R. Constantino (Ed.), *Linguistic Minorities and Literacy: Access and Opportunity.* Lanham, Maryland: Scarecrow Press. In press.

McQuillan, J. and Tse, L. (1997) "Let's talk about books: Using literature circles in second language classrooms." In G. Jacobs, C. Davis and W. Renandya (Eds.), *Successful Strategies for Extensive Reading.* Singapore: SEAMEO Regional Language Centre. pp. 90-97.

Merino, B., Trueba, H. and Sanmaniego, F. (Eds.) (1993) *Language and Culture in Learning: Teaching Spanish to Native Speakers of Spanish.* London: Falmer Press.

Nagy, W., Herman, P. and Anderson, R. (1985) "Learning words from context." *Reading Research Quarterly* **20**: 233–253.

Pucci, S. (1994) "Supporting Spanish language literacy: Latino children and free reading resources in the schools." *Bilingual Research Journal* **18**: 67–82.

Roca, A. (1992) "Spanish for U.S. Hispanic Bilinguals in Higher Education." *ERIC Digest Series* EDO–FL–92–06.

Rodrigo, V. (1994) *Spanish Vocabulary Checklist for Intermediate Students*. Unpublished manuscript, University of Southern California.

Sole, Y. (1994) "The input hypothesis and the bilingual learner." *The Bilingual Review/La Revista Bilingue* **19**: 99–110.

Schon, I., Hopkins, K. and Davis, W.A. (1982) "The effects of books in Spanish and free reading time on Hispanic students' reading abilities and attitudes." *NABE Journal* **7**: 13–20.

Schon, I., Hopkins, K. and Vojir, C. (1984) "The effects of Spanish reading emphasis on the English and Spanish reading abilities of Hispanic high school students." *The Bilingual Review/La Revista Bilingue* **11**: 33–39.

Schon, I., Hopkins, K. and Vojir, C. (1985) "The effects of special reading time in Spanish on the reading abilities and attitudes of Hispanic junior high school students." *Journal of Psycholinguistic Research* **14**: 57–65.

Valdes, G. (1995) "The teaching of minority languages as academic subjects: Pedagogical and theoretical challenges." *Modern Language Journal* **79**: 229–238.

West, R., and Stanovich, K. (1991) "The incidental acquisition of information from reading." *Psychological Science* **2**: 325–330.

7. Do People Appreciate the Benefits of Advanced First Language Development? Attitudes towards Continuing First Language Development after "Transition"

Fay Shin and Stephen Krashen

The arguments for continuing the development of the child's first language after "transition" are well-known: Advanced first language development has practical, career-related advantages (Simon, 1980), and can result in superior cognitive development (Hakuta, 1986). In addition, advanced first language development can increase respect for the first culture and can result in a healthy sense of biculturalism, avoiding the destructive syndrome of "bicultural ambivalence," shame of the first culture and rejection of the second culture (Cummins, 1981). Advanced first language development is thus good for the student and good for society.

Contrary to popular opinion, former limited English proficient students are losing their first language competence rapidly. Garcia and Diaz (1992), for example, reported that 12th graders who began school as monolingual Spanish speakers rated their English writing ability higher than their Spanish writing ability, and reported a preference for English when speaking with siblings.

Planners of first language development programs will profit from knowing public opinion. In this study, we examine the views of several different groups, focussing not only on the overall advisability of such programs, but on reactions to the three advantages cited above.

Procedure

SUBJECTS:

Korean-speaking parents: Data on the views of Korean parents was obtained from Shin and Kim (in press). In their study, 256 parents of children in elementary school were surveyed. Fifty-two percent of the sample had lived in the United States less than eight years, and 63% reported having a college education.

Spanish-speaking parents: Data on the views of Spanish-speaking parents was obtained from Shin and Gribbons (1996). In this study, 150 parents of children in middle school were surveyed. Ninty-three percent had lived in the United States longer than eight years, and more than half (54% of the fathers, 58% of the mothers) had not completed high school.

Hmong-speaking parents: This data was obtained from Shin and Lee (1996), who surveyed 100 parents of Hmong speaking children in grades K through 12. Seventy-three percent of the sample had been in the US less than eight years, and 60% of the fathers and 73% of the mothers had not completed high school.

Students: Additional data from 148 middle school children, ages 11 to 14, was collected. Eighty-eight percent of this sample had lived in the United States more than eight years and only 1% less than one year. Sixty-three percent reported English as their primary language, and only 11% reported currently being in an ESL program.

Teachers: Data from teachers was obtained from Shin and Krashen (1996). In this study, 794 elementary and secondary teachers from the San Joaquin Valley were surveyed. Ninety percent of the sample had been teaching longer than two years, and 66% of the sample said that they had more than 20% limited English proficient students in their classes.

Administrators: Responses from 90 randomly selected administrators (69% principals, 22% assistant principals) from Anton and Shin (1997) were included. Eighty-seven percent of the respondents reported that they had worked in the public schools for more than 10 years, and only 16% reported that they spoke another language.

INSTRUMENT

All subjects filled out a short questionnaire probing attitudes about bilingual education. Versions for Korean and Spanish-speaking parents were translated into the first language. There were slight differences among the questionnaires, but in all cases questions focussed on the rationale for advanced first language development, as well as respondees' opinion of continuing primary language education after students had acquired English.

Response options were slightly different for each sample. All groups of parents, the administrators, and the children simply responded "yes" (agree), "no" (disagree) or "not sure" to each statement, while teachers indicated their agreement and disagreement on a five-point scale. The questions dealt with the following issues:

(1) *Practical advantages:* Parents, administrators and teachers were asked if they thought that "High levels of bilingualism can lead to practical, career-related goals," while children were asked: "Do you believe that being able to speak two languages will help a person in their career and future?"

(2) *Cognitive benefits:* Parents were asked if they agreed that "high levels of bilingualism can result in superior cognitive development." The teachers' and administrators' question was similar: "Do you believe high levels of bilingualism can result in higher development of knowledge or mental skills?" while children were asked: "Do you believe being able to speak two languages very well can make you smarter and broaden your intellectual development?"

(3) *Biculturalism:* This issue was not fully probed with the parents, who were only asked if they agreed that "It is necessary to keep your child's primary language." Teachers and students answered two questions related to this issue. One question simply asked if maintaining the first culture was a good idea (Teachers and administrators: "Do you believe it is good for students to maintain their native culture, as well as American culture?" Students: "Do you believe it is good to maintain your cultural heritage, as well as American culture?") and a second question asked about the role of the first language (Teachers and administrators: "Do you believe the development of the native language helps develop a sense of biculturalism?" Students: "Do you believe the development of a person's first language helps a person maintain and keep two cultures?")

(4) *Continued first language development in school:* The question presented to all groups was very similar. We present here the one on the teacher questionnaire: "If a student is proficient in both Spanish and English, do you believe he/she should be enrolled in a classroom where the first language is part of the curriculum?"

Results

Results are presented in table 1. No statistical analysis was performed, because our goal was not to determine which group was more or less supportive, but to get an idea of overall public support. In addition, there were slight differences in question wording and response options. Despite these differences, our results give a general idea of the level of support for continuing first language development.

Table 1

Comparison of six studies; attitudes toward continued first language development

Percent Agreement	K	S	H	C	T[1]	AD
1. Bilingualism leads to practical, career-related advantage	97	75	86	89	85	87
2. Bilingualism helps cognitive development	86	61	89	68	71	74
3. "necssary to keep primary language"	95	87	88			
4. It is good to maintain the first culture		90	67			91
5. Developing the first language helps maintain the first culture	75	53				61
6. Participation in bilingual program if child is proficient in English	86	59	44	58	43	37

K: Korean parents
S: Spanish parents
H: Hmong parents
C: Children (middle school)
T: Teachers
AD: Administrators
1:    For the teacher group, categories were combined: a response of 4 or 5 out of 5 was considered "agree."

The results in table 1 show strong agreement for the rationale underlying advanced first language development. Apparently, these rationale make good intuitive sense, in addition to being supported by the research. We can expect that support for these principles would be even stronger if these groups were informed about the research.

With the exception of the Korean parents, subjects showed less support for actual participation in programs for continuing first language development (question 6). Apparently, while our subjects clearly do appreciate the value of advanced first language development, they are not agreed that it should be done in school. Aguirre (1984) reported similar results for Mexican American parents: 55% agreed that "the use of Spanish in the bilingual classroom should stop as soon as the Spanish-speaking child learns English." Mexican American teachers, however, supported heritage language development; 80% disagreed with the above statement.

Discussion

Several issues remain unsettled. It is established that speakers of heritage languages often go through a period of rejection of the first culture and language, and may only become interested in their linguistic and cultural heritage in adolescence or adulthood (Tse, this volume). Should we wait for the opportune time, or will well-taught heritage language classes prevent the rejection of the first language and culture?

In addition, the issue of methodology in advanced first language development needs to be addressed. The usual approach to "Spanish for native speakers," for example, is grammar-based, which is in conflict with current theories of literacy and language development. Current theory claims that exposure to comprehensible input in the form of interesting reading and study of current events and history will result in greater language development, including better grammatical accuracy (Krashen, 1982, 1993); studies by McQuillan (this volume) suggest that such an approach can work for intermediate and advanced first language development.

Finally, just how much heritage language instruction is necessary, and how much is even possible in our already overcrowded curriculum? Our goal, we suggest, should be to provide enough so that the student can interact easily with educated native speakers, and read in the first language. This will allow improvement to take place after the program is over. Just how much competence students need to attain this goal is an empirical question, but it is a question that should not be difficult to answer.

References

Aguirre, A. (1984) "Parent and teacher opinions of bilingual education: Comparisons and contrasts." *NABE Journal* **9(1):** 41–51.

Anton, M. and Shin, F. "What do K-12 school principals think about bilingual education?" Forthcoming.

Cummins, J. (1981) "The role of primary language development in promoting success for language minority students." In Office of Bilingual Bicultural Education (Eds.), *Schooling and Language Minority Children: A Theoretical Framework*.   Los Angeles: Evaluation, Dissemination and Assessment Center, California State University. pp. 3–49.

Garcia, R. and Diaz, C. (1992) "The status and use of Spanish and English among Hispanic youth in Dade county (Miami) Florida: A sociolinguistic study." *Language and Education* **6**: 13–32.

Hakuta, K. (1986) *The Mirror of Language: The Debate on Bilingualism*. New York: Basic Books.

Krashen, S. (1982) *Principles and Practice in Second Language Acquisition*. New York: Prentice-Hall.

Krashen, S. (1993) *The Power of Reading*. Englewood, CO: Libraries Unlimited.

Shin, F. and Kim, S. "Korean parent perceptions and attitudes of bilingual education." In R. Endo, C. Park, J. Tsuchida, and A. Agbayani (Eds), *Current Issues in Asian and Pacific American Education*. Covina, CA: Pacific Asian Press. In press.

Shin, F. and Krashen, S. (1996) "Teachers' attitudes towards the principles of bilingual education and toward students' particiation in bilingual programs: Same or different?" *Bilingual Research Journal* **20**: 45–53.

Shin, F. and Lee, B. (1996) "Hmong parents: What do they think about bilingual education?" *Pacific Educational Research Journal* **8**: 65–71.

Shin, F. and Gribbons, B. (1996) "Hispanic parent perceptions and attitudes of bilingual education." *The Journal of Mexican American Educators*. pp. 16–22.

Simon, P. (1980) *The Tongue-Tied American*. New York: Continuum Press.